At Issue

| The Death Penalty

Other Books in the At Issue Series

Cyberwarfare
Domestic Terrorism
The Ethics of WikiLeaks
Gender Politics
Pipelines and Politics
Populism and the Digital Age
Reproductive Rights

At Issue

|The Death Penalty

Megan Manzano, Book Editor

GREENHAVEN PUBLISHING

Published in 2018 by Greenhaven Publishing, LLC
353 3rd Avenue, Suite 255, New York, NY 10010

Copyright © 2018 by Greenhaven Publishing, LLC

First Edition

Articles in Greenhaven Publishing anthologies are often edited for length to meet page
requirements. In addition, original titles of these works are changed to clearly present
the main thesis and to explicitly indicate the author's opinion. Every effort is made to
ensure that Greenhaven Publishing accurately reflects the original intent of the authors.
Every effort has been made to trace the owners of the copyrighted material.

Cover image: AVN Photo Lab/Shutterstock.com

Library of Congress Cataloging-in-Publication Data

Names: Manzano, Megan, editor.
Title: The death penalty / Megan Manzano, book editor.
Description: New York : Greenhaven Publishing, 2018. | Series: At Issue |
  Includes bibliographical references and index. | Audience: Grades 9-12.
Identifiers: LCCN 2017027360| ISBN 9781534502086 (library bound) | ISBN
  9781534502130 (pbk.)
Subjects: LCSH: Capital punishment--United States--Juvenile literature. |
  Capital punishment--Juvenile literature.
Classification: LCC KF9227.C2 D41165 2017 | DDC 364.660973--dc23
LC record available at https://lccn.loc.gov/2017027360

Manufactured in the United States of America

Website: http://greenhavenpublishing.com

Contents

Introduction   **7**

1. For and Against the Death Penalty   **10**
   FlameHorse

2. Moral Arguments Complicate Support of the Death Penalty   **17**
   Jeffrey Howard

3. The *Green Mile* and the Death Penalty in Pop Culture   **22**
   Alyssa Rosenberg

4. The Alarming Cost of a Death Penalty Trial   **26**
   Alex Mayyasi

5. Evidence for the Death Penalty as a Deterrent Is Lacking   **29**
   Carolyn Hoyle and Roger Hood

6. Race and Its Impact on Death Penalty Cases   **33**
   Katherine Beckett and Heather Evans

7. How Gender Affects the Death Penalty   **45**
   Amanda Oliver

8. Misrepresentation in Capital Cases   **50**
   Capital Punishment in Context

9. How State Ordered Executions Challenge Medical Ethics   **61**
   James K. Boehnlein

10. Lethal Injections and the Law   **67**
    Soli Salgado

11. Lethal Injections Aren't More Humane   **73**
    Joel B. Zivot

12. Changing the Code of Ethics Could End the Death Penalty   **81**
    Tara Culp-Ressler

13. Innocent People Can Receive the Death Penalty   **88**
    Nicole Colson

14. The Death Penalty Has Consequences for   **96**
    Families, Too
    Federica Valabrega

15. Problems with Today's Death Penalty System   **104**
    Marc Hyden

16. The Fate of the Death Penalty Abroad   **108**
    Viasna

Organizations to Contact   **111**
Bibliography   **115**
Index   **118**

Introduction

The death penalty dates back to thousands of years BCE, but modern-day governments still use it as a form of punishment. The laws and reasons for the death penalty in the past have varied, anywhere from treason to striking a parent. In more current times, the death penalty is optioned to those with offenses such as murder, terrorism, espionage and the like. In the last two hundred years, it has faced great controversy as governments debate on whether it should be kept or abolished and what the implications of either decision will lead to.

In the nineteenth century, abolishing the death penalty was linked to the abolitionist movement. The outcry led many states to move crime away from public view and instead set up state penitentiaries where the death penalty could still be enacted. In 1838, laws were passed in both Tennessee and Alabama, which allowed for circumstances to be taken into account upon committing a capital crime. This was an important piece of legislation for the death penalty was formerly given to capital crimes regardless of circumstance. The beginning of the twentieth century brought on a period of reform, intended to place limits on the death penalty. Six states outlawed the death penalty while three others only attributed the death penalty to crimes of treason or the murder of a government official. These reforms were short-lived. Fears of violence and revolution followed the Russian Revolution and the United States decision to enter World War I (1914-1918). Instability among social and economic classes threatened a once stable capitalistic system. The death penalty was reinstated in five out of the six states that had formerly outlawed it. Many argued the death penalty was the only way to quell crime. In the 1930's, more people were executed in the United States than in any other time—a total of 167 per year. This change was a product of a chaotic time in history. By the 1950's, support for the death penalty dropped once again.

Many allies of the United States had either outlawed or severely limited the usage of the death penalty. The Universal Declaration of Human Rights had been established in 1948, stating everyone had a right to life. The United Nations insisted the death penalty should be limited. Australia stopped executions in the 1960's and the murder rate fell shortly thereafter. Canada abolished the death penalty in 1976 and saw a spike in homicide, but that too leveled out and was 43% lower in 2003 than it was a year before the death penalty was no longer legal. A similar trend occurred in Central and Eastern Europe, when after abolishing the death penalty and strengthening laws, homicide rates declined. It is difficult to say whether these trends were coincidental or a result of abolishing the death penalty, but there is no way to test capital punishment without running into a variety of moral and ethical problems.

At the same time, as other parts of the world were abolishing this punishment, the United States began questioning the moral implications of the death penalty. This challenged several constitutional amendments. The first case to call the death penalty into question was *US v. Jackson*. It was discussed that the death penalty should be left up to the recommendation of a jury. This ruling was ultimately declined for defendants could deny their right to trial in order to avoid the death penalty. The second case was *Witherspoon v. Illinois*, where it was decided that juror's opinions about the death penalty could not prevent them from serving on a jury. Only if their views on the death penalty would severely impact their judgment could a juror be exempted from serving. Questions continued to arise in the United States behind the legalities of the death penalty, whether it was right or wrong to execute a mentally ill person or a minor. The former was outlawed in the 1980's while the latter was not fully outlawed until 2005. Innocence of a criminal was also brought up, though Courts insisted such cases would be rare occurrences. To this day, there is still no perfect system for seeking out those who are innocent except for evidence presented in a trial.

Support for the death penalty was highest in the United States in 1990, drawing an overall 80 percent approval rating. Percentages have dropped to roughly 60 percent in recent years, but opinions on the death penalty still remain conflicted. Life without parole is growing to be a favored sentence when it comes to those convicted of murder; 46 percent favor life imprisonment instead of the death penalty, while 62 percent are skeptical on whether the death penalty actually influences a lower crime rate. There is a lot to consider about the death penalty. Inmates are no longer executed by the electric chair. They instead receive a lethal injection. Many have argued that this breaks a doctor's oath as they are not trying to maintain life, but rather take it away. What must also be looked at are the influences that can affect a death penalty sentence. Those of low economic status are more likely to receive the death penalty, as are criminals of color for they do not have access to good lawyers or legal help. People with mental illness, too, fall under this bracket, for they are often put in prison as opposed to receiving the proper health care they require to live. Death penalty sentences are not always clear cut. Every person receives a different sentence, even if they commit the same crime. Therefore the definition of what makes a case a death penalty case is arbitrary. If one is sentenced to death, factors of state cost and the suffering of one's family weigh heavily on the decision. Some, however, believe that the death penalty is worth all of these setbacks if crime will be deterred and those who commit the worst offenses will receive the correct punishment.

As the viewpoints in *At Issue: The Death Penalty* describe, the death penalty debate is still a very heated discussion.

1

For and Against the Death Penalty

FlameHorse

FlameHorse is the nom de plume of a freelance writer for Listverse and Imgur who covers history, religion and current events. He claims to be a pacifist who loves animals and eats burgers.

It is not always clear whether the death penalty is implemented so inmates can be rehabilitated or so retribution can be taken against them. As the following five for-and-against arguments illustrate, a slew of reasons exist on both sides of the debate, opening up questions as to how legal systems handle victim closure, crime deterrence, medical cruelty and prison reform.

The existence of the death penalty in any society raises one underlying question: have we established our justice systems out of a desire for rehabilitation, or out of a desire for retribution?

The lister has set out to examine both sides of the debate over the ethics and legality of capital punishment, especially in the US, and chooses neither side in any of the following entries. They are not presented in any meaningful order.

Against: It Teaches the Condemned Nothing

What is the purpose of punishment? We take our lead from one major source, our parents—and they no doubt took their lead from their own parents. When your young child emulates what he just

"5 Arguments For And Against The Death Penalty," by Flamehorse, List Verse Ltd., June 1, 2013. Reprinted by Permission.

saw in a Rambo movie, you give him a stern lecture about what is real and what is not, what is acceptable in real life and what is not. When your child tries some crazy acrobatic move off a piece of furniture and hurts himself, you might spank him to be sure that he remembers never to do it again.

So when the child grows up, breaks into a home, and steals electronics, he gets caught and goes to prison. His time in prison is meant to deprive him of the freedom to go where he wants anywhere in the world, and to do what he wants when he wants. This is the punishment, and most people do learn from it. In general, no one wants to go back. But if that child grows up and murders someone for their wallet or just for fun, and they are in turn put to death, they are taught precisely nothing, because they are no longer alive to learn from it. We cannot rehabilitate a person by killing him or her.

For: It is the Ultimate Warning

Nevertheless, if would-be criminals know undoubtedly that they will be put to death should they murder with premeditation, very many of them are much less inclined to commit murder. Whether or not would-be criminals are wary of committing the worst crime is an important—and probably impossible—question to answer. Murder still happens very frequently. So some criminals disregard this warning for various reasons. But the fact does remain that many criminals who ride the fence on committing murder ultimately decide to spare the victim's life.

In a larger sense, capital punishment is the ultimate warning against all crimes. If the criminal knows that the justice system will not stop at putting him to death, then the system appears more draconian to him. Hence, he is less inclined to break and enter. He may have no intention of killing anyone in the process of robbing them, but is much more apprehensive about the possibility if he knows he will be executed. Thus, there is a better chance that he will not break and enter in the first place.

Against: It Does Not Dissuade

If the foreknowledge of any punishment is meant to dissuade the criminal from committing the crime, why do people still murder others? The US had a 2012 murder rate of 4.8 victims per 100,000—meaning that nearly 15,000 people were victims of homicide that year. Capital punishment does not appear to be doing its job; it doesn't seem to be changing every criminal's mind about killing innocent people. If it does not dissuade, then it serves no purpose. The warning of life in prison without parole must equally dissuade criminals.

For: It Provides Closure for Victims

There are many victims of a single murder. The criminal gets caught, tried, and convicted, and it is understood that the punishment will be severe. But the person he has killed no longer has a part to play in this. Unfortunately, the murderer has deprived his family and friends of a loved one. Their grief begins with the murder. It may not end with the murderer's execution, but the execution does engender a feeling of relief at no longer having to think about the ordeal—a feeling which often fails to arise while the murderer still lives on.

A system in place for the purpose of granting justice cannot do so for the surviving victims, unless the murderer himself is put to death.

Against: It is Hypocritical

It is strange that a nation would denounce the practice of murder by committing the very same act. By doing so, we're essentially championing the right to life by taking it from others. True—as a whole, we are not murderers, and understandably refuse to be placed in the same category as someone like Ted Bundy. But to many opponents of the death penalty, even Ted Bundy should have been given life without parole. The fact that he murdered at least thirty people—for the mere reason that he enjoyed doing it—has no bearing on the hypocrisy, the flagrant dishonesty, of the declaration that such a person deserves to be killed because he had no right to kill.

If the goal of any punishment, as stated above, is to teach us those things we should not do, then the justice system should more adequately teach the criminality of killing by refusing to partake in it.

For: It is All That Would-be Criminals Fear

If you read about Bundy's life in prison, waiting nine years for his execution, you will see that the man exhausted every single legal point he and his lawyers could think of, all in an attempt to spare him execution. He "defended" himself in prison interviews by blaming pornography for causing his uncontrollable teenage libido, and for causing him to think of women as objects and not humans. He attempted to have his death sentence commuted to life without parole by explaining that it was all pornography's fault, and that had it never existed, he would have been a good person.

When that didn't work, he pretended to come clean and tell police where the bodies of unfound victims were, so that their families could have closure. He never once admitted that he was a bad person, and just before his execution, he claimed that he hadn't done anything wrong. It was obvious that he feared being put to death. He did his best to avert it.

This means that he did not fear life in prison—at least not as much as he feared capital punishment. He had many opportunities to kill himself in his cell, but he did not. He might have done it a month before his execution, when all hope for clemency was gone—but he was afraid of death. How many would-be murderers have turned away at the last second purely out of fear of the executioner's needle?

Against: It is Always Cruel

In the end, though, death is always at least a little painful. Perhaps the only truly peaceful way to go is while asleep—but no one has ever come back to say that this didn't hurt. If your heart stops while you sleep, it is certainly possible that your brain will recognize a problem and wake you up at the very moment when it is too late. So what we cannot help but let Nature do, we ought not to force on others for any reason. If we do so, it might be fair to say that we law-abiding people, who embody the justice system, are guilty of equal cruelty towards criminals who commit murder. The United Nations' Universal Declaration of Human Rights, for one, dictates that "no one shall be subjected to torture or to cruel, inhuman or degrading treatment or punishment."

In the US, there are five legal methods of execution: lethal injection, electrocution, firing squad, hanging, and gassing. These are all intended to be as painless as possible, but they all run the risk of accidents. John Wayne Gacy, who was not afraid of death, was executed via lethal injection—the most efficient, risk-free method. Yet his death did not go as planned.

The sodium thiopental entered his bloodstream successfully and put him to sleep. The pancuronium bromide was then administered successfully to paralyze his diaphragm. This would cause asphyxiation if the next chemical, potassium chloride, were not immediately administered to stop the heart. But the potassium chloride had congealed in its tube before Gacy was brought into the room. He was unconscious and unable to breathe for several minutes while the last drug's tube was changed. His death took eighteen minutes, instead of the usual seven. And whether or not he was in great pain is impossible to determine.

For: It is Not Always Cruel

It's true that cruelty should not be legally tolerated—and the five methods listed above are very efficient in killing the condemned before he or she is able to feel it. Granted, we are not able to ask the dead whether or not they felt their necks snap, or the chemicals burn inside them—but modern American executions very rarely go awry. It does happen, but the reported accidents since 1976 number about ten nationwide, out of 1,328.

When the condemned is fastened into the electric chair, one of the conductors is strapped securely around the head with the bare metal flush against the shaved and wet scalp. This permits the electricity to be conducted directly into the brain, shutting it off more quickly than the brain can register pain.

Hanging causes death by snapping the neck of the condemned around the second vertebrae—instantly shutting off the brain's ability to communicate with the rest of the body, and causing the heart to stop within seconds.

The firing squad involves five men shooting the heart of the condemned with high-powered rifles. The heart is completely destroyed and unconsciousness follows within seconds.

The gas chamber is now no longer forced on the condemned, because it frequently appeared to cause more pain than was expected or acceptable. The gas is usually hydrogen cyanide, which inhibits mitochondrial respiration in every cell of the entire body, theoretically shutting off the brain like a light switch. But it requires that the condemned breathe deeply.

Against: Prison is Hell on Earth

Consider a pedophile who kills an infant girl by raping her. There is an unwritten "code of honor" in prisons that virtually requires inmates to kill such offenders. Probably half of America's prisoners were in some way abused as children, and harbor a seething hatred for those who abuse children. The murdering pedophile is given the death penalty, but will probably spend ten years beforehand in prison. He will most likely be housed in solitary confinement for his own protection, but there are frequently holes in such protection, and the inmates may find their way to him. And if this happens, pedophiles are often gang-raped, castrated, beaten to death, stabbed, and sometimes even beheaded before guards—who may deliberately ignore the scene—can save them.

Most prisoners consider each other to be in the same predicament, and treat each other quite well in general. But they are still in prison, and despair about their lack of freedom. What is life like for Zacarias Moussaoui, the member of the September 11 hijacking teams who got caught a month before the attack? A single juror saved him from death. He has, since 2006, been incarcerated for twenty-three hours per day in a tiny concrete cell, with one hour of daily exercise in an empty concrete swimming pool; he has no access to other inmates, and only rare contact with guards, who say nothing to him; he can see nothing of the outside world except a tiny sliver of sky—and this will be his life. Capital punishment is an unnecessary threat.

For: It is the Best Answer to Murder

The justice system basically attempts to mete out punishment that fits the crime. Severe crimes result in imprisonment. "Petty larceny" is not treated with the severity that is meted to "grand theft auto," and the latter, consequently, receives more time in prison. So if severe—but non-lethal—violence toward another is found deserving of life without parole, then why should premeditated homicide be given the very same punishment? This fact might induce a would-be criminal to go ahead and kill the victim he has already mugged and crippled. Why would it matter, after all? His sentence could not get any worse.

If murder is the willful deprivation of a victim's right to life, then the justice system's willful deprivation of the criminal's right to the same is—even if overly severe—a punishment which fits the most severe crime that can be committed. Without capital punishment, it could be argued that the justice system makes no provision in response to the crime of murder, and thus provides no justice for the victim.

2

Moral Arguments Complicate Support of the Death Penalty

Jeffrey Howard

Jeffrey Howard is a lecturer in political philosophy at Essex University. He is based in the Department of Government, where he teaches ethics and public policy, the history of political thought, and contemporary political philosophy.

Worldviews differ on the death penalty, with some nations in Europe pushing for inmate reform, while the United States continues to support the usage of capital punishment—albeit with measures like lethal injection. Meanwhile, countries like India still go the "old-fashioned" route and hang their condemned prisoners. Reform, deterrence and retribution play a large role in the global conversation when it comes to choosing to keep the death penalty or abolish it. In order to understand the main arguments of the death penalty, philosophical and moral ideas from different cultures and religions must be taken into account, too.

The execution, by hanging, of Yakub Memon for his part in the 2003 Mumbai bombings invites us to revisit the vexed issue of capital punishment. Few topics incite such moral passion and controversy.

"Death penalty: is capital punishment morally justified?" by Jeffrey Howard, The Conversation, August 1, 2015. https://theconversation.com/death-penalty-is-capital-punishment-morally-justified-42970. CC BY-ND 4.0 International.

The world's religious communities are divided on the death penalty. Despite a seemingly unambiguous commitment to non-violence (or "Ahimsa") in both Hinduism and Buddhism, scholars within those traditions continue to debate the permissibility of lethal punishment. The Old Testament enjoins us to take an "eye for an eye"—the principle of *lex talionis*—while the New Testament exhorts us to "turn the other cheek". And while Islam is generally regarded as compatible with the death penalty, the Qur'an's emphasis on forgiveness suggests that Muslims should sometimes respond to evil with mercy, not retaliation.

While many European countries urge an ethic of rehabilitation in their criminal justice systems, many jurisdictions in the United States stand firmly in favour of capital punishment for serious crimes. Even a federal jury in Massachusetts, a liberal bastion, recently doled out the death penalty to the sole surviving perpetrator of the Boston marathon bombing. And while the United Kingdom abandoned the death penalty in 1964—the year of the last executions—nearly half of the British public favours a reintroduction of it (though that figure has been dropping steadily).

We will not make progress in the public debate about the death penalty unless we realise that it is only one element in a much bigger controversy: about the point of punishment itself. As The Conversation invites us to rethink the death penalty over the next few weeks, we must not conduct this discussion in a vacuum. Before you ask yourself whether we should have the death penalty, consider: why hand out any punishments at all? Considering the three main families in the philosophy of punishment can help us organise our conversation.

Retribution

"Bad guys deserve to suffer." This is a blunt slogan, but it captures the essence of a deeply familiar notion: people who have committed culpable wrongs deserve their lives to go worse as a result. Why do they deserve it? Perhaps because it's not fair for the lives of wrongdoers to go well when the lives of the innocent have gone poorly—punishment levels the playing field. Whatever the reason, "retributivists"—those who believe in retribution—argue that the punishment of criminals is *intrinsically* valuable; it is valuable in and of itself, rather than valuable because of its good consequences (for example, preventing future crime).

Even if punishing murderers and thieves had no effect on reducing the overall crime rate, retributivists tend to think it's still the right thing to do. Retributivists also think that the severity of punishment should match the severity of the crime. So, just as it is wrong to over-punish someone (executing someone for stealing a pair of shoes), it can be wrong to under-punish someone (giving him a community service order for murder).

If you are a retributivist, you might support the death penalty because you think that certain or all murderers (and perhaps other criminals) deserve to suffer death for their crimes. Depending on how you think about death, however, you might oppose the death penalty on the grounds that it is disproportionately harsh—perhaps you think that no matter what someone has done, she does not deserve to die for it.

On the other hand you might oppose the death penalty on the grounds that it is disproportionately light. Many people who opposed the recent death sentence for the Boston bomber did so on the grounds that life in a maximum-security prison would be a worse punishment—and so more fitting—than death.

Deterrence

"Criminals should be punished so that they and others will be less likely to commit crime in the future, making everybody safer." Many people criticise retributivism on the grounds that it is nothing but a pointless quest for barbaric revenge.

Inflicting suffering on human beings, if it is to be morally justified, must instead have a forward-looking purpose: protecting the innocent from harm. If this sounds sensible to you, you probably believe the point of punishment is not retribution, but rather deterrence.

The idea here is familiar enough: people face temptations to break just laws; the demands of morality and the demands of rational self-interest sometimes seem to diverge. Threats of punishment realign those demands by making it irrational for self-interested individuals to break the law.

If you are a defender of deterrence, you must answer two questions about capital punishment before determining where you stand. The first is empirical: a question about real-world facts. Does the threat of the death penalty actually deter people from committing heinous crimes to a greater extent than the threat of life imprisonment?

The second question is moral. Even if the death penalty deterred crime more successfully than life imprisonment, that doesn't necessarily mean it would be justified. After all, imagine if we threatened execution for all crimes, including minor traffic violations, theft, and tax fraud.

Doing so would surely slash the crime rate, yet most people would judge it to be wrong. Deterrence theorists tend to defend some upper limit on the harshness of punishment—and it may be that death simply goes beyond what the government is ever permitted to threaten.

Reform

"Punishment communicates to criminals that what they have done is wrong, and gives them an opportunity to apologise and reform." There are many different variants of this view: educative, communicative, rehabilitative—and there are important differences between them. But the basic idea is that punishment should make the wrongdoer understand what he or she has done wrong and inspire her to repent and reform.

Whatever version of this view one supports, its implication for the death penalty is reasonably clear. What is the point of a criminal reforming herself as she prepares for the execution chamber?

To be sure, many people try to mix and match different elements of these three broad views, though such mixed theories tend to be unhelpfully *ad hoc* and can offer conflicting guidance. Far better, to my mind, to plant one's flag clearly and answer the question: which view should have priority in our thinking about punishment?

Then, and only then, can we proceed to think about the justice (or lack thereof) of governments who kill their citizens.

3

The Green Mile and the Death Penalty in Pop Culture

Alyssa Rosenberg

Alyssa Rosenberg is a writer on politics and culture for the Washington Post.

The 1999 film The Green Mile, based on the serialized novel by Stephen King, still resonates today as a commentary on capital punishment. The story of guards faced with a miracle-performing prisoner on Death Row in a small Louisiana penitentiary, it forces its audience to take a look at how distance and a lack of responsibility allow opinions to form in favor of the death penalty. Even if the justice system was not affected by race, gender, sexuality, or class, it is hard to say whether these opinions would be correct—but The Green Mile certainly doesn't soften the denizens of Death Row or their crimes.

In the comments thread in last week's conversation, I confessed some ambivalence about the position that I've staked out here: that it makes more sense to set the standard for conversation about the death penalty that it should be abolished in all circumstances, even in the astonishingly unlikely chance that we achieve a perfectly just criminal justice system that has no clear disparate impact on people of any rage, gender, class, or creed. I say that not because I think we're more likely to achieve a durable opposition to the death penalty by relaying on pragmatic arguments rather than

"Pop Culture and the Death Penalty Project: 'The Green Mile,'" by Alyssa Rosenberg, ThinkProgress, October 27, 2011. Reprinted by Permission.

moral ones—I think it may initially seem easier to bring people in with pragmatic arguments, but that may not achieve the depth of consensus we hope for. But rather, I confess some ambivalence because I have never been the victim of a violent crime, and I've had the good fortune that no one in my family has been touched by violent crime either. I'd like to believe that if such a thing were to come to pass, I would resist the urge to take another person's life, but I'm afraid that I wouldn't, that the better angels of my nature would be decisively scattered and I would want what I now profess to abhor. Which I suppose is as good an argument for total abolition as any: if we can't trust ourselves in moments of extremism, perhaps some tools should be taken away from us.

But on to *The Green Mile*. It's a fascinating—and very sentimental movie—and to a certain extent, it's not particularly useful as a basis for a real-world conversation about the death penalty. People who perform executions may have the experience of helping to kill innocent people—we know some of them certainly have. But they're deeply unlikely to execute people who are not only innocent but honest-to-god saintly miracle workers who absolve them on the way to the electric chair, telling them, as John tells Paul, "You tell God the father it was a kindness you done." But the movie is an intermittently powerful allegory about responsibility, and the way we distance ourselves from culpability and full understanding of what we're doing.

That distance is part of the way Paul explains his work to his elderly listener, and to himself. "Death row was usually called the Last Mile. We called ours the Green Mile," he says. "The floor was the color of faded limes. We had the electric chair. Old Sparky, we called it." These are cute names for terrible things, the wait for your death at the hands of the state, the instrument of your death, which even when it goes well, is an ugly, traumatic thing—and far worse when your death is sabotaged by a sadistic prison guard. But the characters struggle with the distance that lets them do their day-to-day jobs, and the need to honestly confront what they do when they take a man's life. We know Percy is disgusting not just because he's cruel, but because when he deliberately sabotages an execution in a way that makes the man's death prolonged and hideously painful, he tries not to witness what he's wrought. By contrast, we feel sympathy with, not disgust for, Paul when he hesitates to give the order to execute John because he's meditated on the terrible work he's about to perform. His sense of duty and his sense of right conflict. And when we learn Paul is living out a vastly extended life because "It's my torment. It's my punishment for letting John Coffey ride the light," I can't help but wonder if he'd be tormented in the same way if he'd executed anyone else.

But the movie is much more muddled about the justice of executing people who aren't innocent, or of doing terrible things to terrible people. Wild Bill is a terrible person, whether he's murdering small children or harassing and assaulting people who are attempting to do their jobs and treat him decently. It's hard to feel very sorry for him when he's placed in solitary confinement in a straightjacket, hosed down with a firehose, or ultimately, shot by a possessed Percy. Similarly, when the guards put Percy in the straitjacket and confine him, with a gag taped in his mouth, so they can take John to the Warden's house to heal his daughter, it's hard to think of another option they might have had. And while it's framed as an uncomfortable event, it's mostly uncomfortable because there's a risk Percy will rat them out, not because what they're doing to this deeply stunted man is wrong. And at the end of the movie, when he winds up institutionalized, it's hard to feel more sympathy for him than relief from the people who are safe for him.

In fact, I was struck by how the movie makes active pragmatic arguments for why it makes sense for the guards to behave decently, and passive ones for why it's morally right. "You'd do better to think of this place as an intensive care hospital," Paul warns Percy, suggesting that guards will be less likely to be injured on the job if the inmates are kept calm. "I think of it as a bucket of piss to drown rats in," Percy spits back, unable to weigh his lust for cruelty against the prospect of others' injury. And of course Paul is right. But some of the movie's most moving sequences come as the guards prepare Del for his execution, playing with his mouse and promising that they'll take care of it after his death, a kindness that costs them nothing, and does no harm, but that makes their experiences with Del, his last contributions on earth, about decency and amusement rather than cruelty. It doesn't make up for the murder he committed. But then, nothing can.

4

The Alarming Cost of a Death Penalty Trial

Alex Mayyasi

Alex Mayyasi is a writer, editor, and reporter. Most recently, he was an editor of Priceonomics, a media startup in San Francisco.

In 1972, the Supreme Court declared that rulings for the death penalty required a second trial to determine if death was the appropriate punishment. A death penalty trial costs the state millions of dollars more than a non-capital punishment trial or a term in prison. They also cost a lot more time as these trials require expert witnesses, an extremely vetted jury, and are more likely to have appeals. Does this provide an argument against capital punishment as a whole, or just indicate that the current system needs an overhaul?

A death penalty trial costs the state that pursues it millions of dollars more than a non-capital trial. In other words, it costs more to execute a criminal in the United States than to lock him up in prison for life.

The roots of this surprising fact include that death row inmates must be held in expensive maximum security prisons (which require that inmates be in solitary cells and supervised 24/7) and that the methods of execution, such as lethal injection, have been challenged in court as inhumane. But the main reason is that court cases seeking the death penalty cost more than an ordinary trial:

they take more time, require the jury be more carefully vetted, necessitate more expert witnesses, and invite more appeals.

Investigating the mystery of why executing a man would cost more than imprisoning him for life, we expressed some alarm that capital cases receive so much more attention. Spending extra time to be certain about the guilt of someone sentenced to death is a worthy goal. But life imprisonment without parole is also a serious sentence. Should cases seeking only life imprisonment really receive less attention than a capital case?

For answers, we turned to Richard Dieter, Executive Director of the Death Penalty Information Center. He explained that the difference in cost is a result of a difference in process rather than quality. "In a typical criminal case, 95% are settled by plea bargain and the sentence is prescribed by law." In contrast, Dieter told us, cases seeking capital punishment "almost always go to jury. They have two trials—one for guilt and one for punishment—and each can be appealed."

The difference in process is a result of the Supreme Court repeatedly ruling that "death is different." As such, courts need to go beyond normal due process to determine that execution is an appropriate punishment. A 1972 Supreme Court case had found that the inconsistent and arbitrary application of the death penalty across the country was unconstitutional and constituted cruel and unusual punishment, therefore necessitating a second trial to determine whether the death penalty is appropriate, as well as additional pre-trial motions, the hiring of more experts, and more time spent scrutinizing the biases of the jurors—all of which increase the duration and cost of the court case. Not to mention the lengthy appeals process which drags on until many prisoners have died of natural causes on death row.

While we were reassured that the resources spent on capital cases did not mean that other criminal cases received less attention, Mr. Dieter and the Death Penalty Information Center do stress that the death penalty system is using billions of dollars that could be put toward other purposes. A report from California demonstrates the huge costs involved:

> "The report found that the state was spending $137 million per year on the death penalty. The Commission estimated a comparable system that sentenced the same inmates to a maximum punishment of life without parole would cost only $11.5 million per year. Since the number of executions in California has averaged less than one every two years since the death penalty was reinstated in 1977, the cost for each execution is over $250 million. The state has also indicated it needs another $400 million to construct a new death row."

California spends an extra $100 million a year on its capital punishment system. But the problem is not unique to California. A report from the Urban Institute found that Maryland spent $186 million on execution cases from 1978 to 1999. A study in Nevada found that the 80 capital cases taking place in just one county would cost $15 million more than they would as normal criminal cases. For counties that decide to seek the death penalty in a case, the financial impact is often comparable to an environmental disaster, forcing the local government to raise taxes or cut public services.

Decisions on the legality and process of execution cases has been and will continue to be based on arguments about justice, not economic grounds. All the same, the financial costs of the death penalty are enormous.

5

Evidence for the Death Penalty as a Deterrent Is Lacking

Carolyn Hoyle and Roger Hood

Professor Carolyn Hoyle is director of the Centre for Criminology. She has published empirical and theoretical research on a number of criminological topics including domestic violence, policing, restorative justice, the death penalty, and wrongful convictions. Roger Hood is a professor emeritus in criminology at the University of Oxford and an emeritus of Fellow of All Souls College. He has written on penal history, race discrimination in sentencing, and parole.

Some countries believe the death penalty is the only method to deter people from crimes such as illegal drug trading or political violence, but empirical data on whether or not capital punishment deters these sorts of crimes is hard to come by. Experimentation with the uses for capital punishment treads a morally questionable line and does not guarantee that any changes to the mind of a person who fully supports the death penalty. According to the viewpoint below, across-the-board clemency for those on death row is also not an effective response.

Australia has executed no-one for half a century. Following the abolition of the death penalty by various states, the federal government abolished capital punishment in 1973.

Nevertheless, Australian citizens—like all of those from abolitionist jurisdictions—face the death penalty when they commit serious crimes in countries that retain it. Bali Nine pair Andrew Chan and Myuran Sukumaran are facing execution in Indonesia following their convictions on drug trafficking charges almost ten years ago. On Saturday, they and seven others were given official notice that they will be killed by firing squad on the prison island of Nusakambangan. Under Indonesian law, the minimum period between receiving notice and execution is 72 hours.

Indonesian President Joko Widodo, popularly known as Jokowi, has insisted all along that he will reject clemency petitions for drug traffickers on death row. In January, six were executed—five of them foreigners—straining Indonesia's diplomatic relations with Brazil and the Netherlands. These countries abolished the death penalty in the 19th century.

Jokowi claims that Indonesia is in the grip of a national drug "emergency". He argues that it needs to execute drug offenders to deter others and thereby reduce the rate of deaths following illicit or illegal drug use. However, he, like others who support the death penalty, can produce no evidence to support this claim.

Because it would be morally repugnant to conduct random experiments in the use of capital punishment, it remains difficult—if not impossible—to find empirical data on the deterrent effects of the threat of capital punishment that would persuade a committed proponent of the death penalty to change their mind.

As far as some crimes punishable by death in several countries are concerned—such as importing or trading in illegal drugs, economic crimes, or politically motivated violence—there is no reliable evidence of the deterrent effects of executions. What evidence there is—which is mostly from the US—should lead any dispassionate analyst to conclude that it is not prudent to accept the hypothesis that capital punishment deters murder to a marginally greater extent than does the supposedly lesser punishment of life imprisonment.

One rather unsophisticated way of considering deterrence is to analyse homicide rates before and after the death penalty is abolished. This at least can show whether countries that abolish capital punishment inevitably experience more murders, as those who support the deterrent argument claim.

In Australia, where the last executions occurred in the mid-1960s, the reported murder rate has, a few fluctuations aside, fallen.

Prior to the abolition of the death penalty in Canada in 1976, the reported homicide rate had been rising. But in 2003, 27 years after abolition, the rate was 43% lower than it was in 1975, the year before abolition.

Likewise, the homicide rate in countries of Central and Eastern Europe declined by about 60% after abolition in the 1990s. In most countries, abolition, and a strengthening of the rule of law, results in a decline in the homicide rate.

While recent studies on deterrence in the US are inconclusive as a whole, and many suffer from methodological problems, they do not produce credible evidence on deterrence as a behavioural mechanism.

Therefore, the issue is not whether the death penalty deters some—if only a few—people where the threat of a lesser punishment would not. Instead, it is whether, when all the circumstances surrounding its use are taken into account, the death penalty is associated with a marginally lower rate of the death penalty-eligible crimes than the next most severe penalty, life imprisonment. There is no evidence that it is.

As far as Indonesia's claims for a deterrent effect are concerned, Oxford scholar Claudia Stoicescu has shown that this claim is based on inaccurate statistics on the number of drug users that need rehabilitation and the number of young people that die each day as a result of drug use.

Quite simply, rigorous analysis of the available data does not support the claims made for the need to retain the death penalty to reduce social harms.

About half of the people on death row in Indonesia have been convicted of drug-related offences. Many are foreigners.

Secrecy surrounds the administration of the death penalty in Indonesia. Prisoners learn about the exact time of their execution only 72 hours in advance.

Australian Prime Minister Tony Abbott and Foreign Minister Julie Bishop have not been able to persuade Jokowi that his belief in deterrence is misguided. However, they could perhaps remind him that his apparent approach to clemency is in breach of Indonesia's binding obligations under Article 6(2) of the International Covenant on Civil and Political Rights. Indonesia became a party to this in 2006.

Clemency should always be considered on a case-by-case basis for each and every prisoner. Jokowi's statement that he will reject clemency for all prisoners sentenced to death for drug offences is in clear contradiction of that principle.

6

Race and Its Impact on Death Penalty Cases

Katherine Beckett and Heather Evans

Katherine Beckett is a professor in the Department of Sociology and the Law, Societies, and Justice Program at the University of Washington. At the time of publication, Heather Evans was a Ph.D Candidate in the Department of Sociology at the University of Washington.

In the following viewpoint, researchers Beckett and Evans take an academic look at how people of color are highly discriminated against in the justice system—which can account for a high number of executions and those waiting to be executed. Studies have been conducted showing that if a white person and a black person committed the same crime, the latter would likely face a worse punishment than the former. In order to understand the death penalty, one must also understand race in society.

Introduction

Although the number of executions taking place in the United States has declined considerably in recent years,[1] capital punishment remains shrouded in controversy.[2] Concerns about "the ultimate sanction" include the high cost of its administration, the apparent arbitrariness of its application, the possibility that available techniques cause considerable pain and suffering, and evidence that the system is "fraught with error."[3] The role of race in capital sentencing is also the subject of much discussion and

"Race, Death, and Justice: Capital Sentencing in Washington State, 1981-2014," Katherine Beckett, Heather Evans, *Columbia Journal of Race and Law*, Volume 6, Issue 2, 2016. https://cjrl.columbia.edu/article/race-death-and-justice/. CC BY 4.0

debate.[4] Indeed, although contemporary death penalty statutes were ostensibly designed to reduce arbitrariness and discrimination in capital sentencing,[5] researchers have nonetheless found that race and other extra-legal factors continue to play a significant role in determining which capital defendants live and which die in the post-Furman era.[6] In particular, there is strong evidence that the race of murder victims influences the administration of the death penalty: many studies find that defendants accused of killing Whites are significantly more likely to be sentenced to death than similarly situated defendants accused of killing Blacks.[7] About a third of the studies investigating capital sentencing processes since 1990 also find that the race of the defendant continues to impact outcomes in capital cases,[8] even as overt and intentional forms of racism decline.[9]

To date, however, no published study has examined the role of race in capital sentencing in Washington State, where the death penalty is now a potential outcome in a very small proportion of all homicide cases. Washington State's current death penalty statute was enacted in 1981 and notably limits the proportion of homicide cases in which the death penalty is a possible outcome.[10] Under the Revised Code of Washington ("RCW"), Chapter 10.95, the death penalty may only be sought if the defendant is convicted of first-degree murder and at least one of fourteen aggravating circumstances is found to exist.[11] By contrast, many death penalty states define a larger category of cases as death-eligible. As a result, these states tend to have larger death row populations and have executed a comparatively large number of defendants than is the case in Washington State.

[...]

In the first, least restrictive category of states, state law authorizes capital punishment for offenses other than first-degree murder and/or in all first-degree murder cases. In Florida, for example, conviction of first-degree murder, felony murder, capital drug trafficking, and capital sexual battery may result in a death sentence. A second, moderately restrictive group of states limit capital punishment to murder cases but, unlike Washington State, treat non-aggravated and/or non-first-degree murder cases as death-eligible. In Missouri, for example, all first-degree homicides are death-eligible (i.e., no aggravating circumstances are required). Some of these states (such as Colorado) also define first-degree murder broadly, to include non-intentional forms of homicide such as felony murder and death caused by "extreme indifference."[13]

The third, most restrictive group of states, which includes Washington, limits capital punishment to aggravated and first-degree murders. That is, prosecutors must prove beyond a reasonable doubt that the defendant committed first-degree murder and that one or more statutorily defined aggravators exist. Among these states, the number of statutory aggravators varies. In general, the more aggravating circumstances, the larger the share of murder cases that are likely to qualify as "aggravated" murder.[14] Unlike Washington, many of the states in this category have expanded the number of aggravating circumstances or otherwise broadened their death penalty statute in recent years.[15] In Pennsylvania, for instance, eighteen aggravated circumstances render a homicide death-eligible; in Tennessee, the statute now identifies seventeen aggravating circumstances.[16]

However, it is not just the number of aggravators that increases the number of death-eligible cases; some aggravators have broader applicability than others. For example, although Colorado's statute identifies only a slightly larger number (seventeen) of aggravators than does Washington State law (fourteen), a recent study found that over ninety percent of Colorado's first-degree murder cases met the statutory definition of aggravated murder and involved death-eligible defendants.[17] By contrast, just 13.3% of Washington State's first-degree murder defendants were convicted of aggravated murder and were death-eligible.[18] As a result of its relatively narrow statutory framework, the number of executions and the size of the death row population are comparatively small in Washington. At present, nine men are on death row in Washington. Only seven of the thirty-three states with prisoners awaiting execution have smaller death row populations,[19] and only eleven have conducted fewer executions since 1976.[20]

The fact that Washington's statutory framework limits the applicability and use of capital punishment is of great importance: statutory schemes that do not sufficiently narrow the class of cases that are death-eligible create the potential for a high degree of arbitrariness and discrimination in the administration of capital punishment.[21] In a number of cases adjudicated since Furman,[22] the Court has ruled that capital sentencing statutes avoid the related problems of over-inclusiveness and arbitrariness if they "genuinely narrow the class of persons eligible for the death penalty."[23] As Marceau concludes, "the constitutionally required narrowing [of death-eligibility] must occur at the legislative level in order to limit the unchecked discretion of prosecutors in deciding whom to prosecute under a statute."[24] Because Washington State's statutory framework does meaningfully narrow the class of homicide cases that are death-eligible, analysis of the role of race in capital cases in Washington is especially instructive: evidence that race matters even where discretion is comparatively constrained would suggest that narrowing the death penalty statute will not necessarily eliminate the role of race in the adjudication of capital cases.

Despite its comparatively limited use, the administration of capital punishment in Washington State remains controversial.[25] In part, this is because federal courts have overturned eight of eleven capital cases after defendants lost their appeals.[26] But the racial composition of persons on Washington's death row is also controversial.[27] At present, four of the nine (forty-four percent) men on death row are Black, despite the fact that the percentage of African Americans in the state population has hovered between three to four percent for decades.[28]

[...]

Race and the Death Penalty: Past and Present

Historically, the use of capital punishment in the United States was bound up with various racialized systems of control, including extra-legal violence. As legal scholar Charles Ogletree, Jr. puts it, "the racially disproportionate application of the death penalty can be seen as being in historical continuity with the long and sordid history of lynching in this country."[31] Although it is tempting to imagine this continuity solely in historical terms, numerous studies indicate that race has continued to influence the administration of capital punishment in locales across the country since its reinstatement in the late 1970s and early 1980s.[32] Some of these studies analyze data regarding the administration of capital punishment from particular jurisdictions within the United States.[33] Others use experimental methods to investigate how the race of hypothetical defendants, victims, and/or jurors impact mock jurors' deliberations and sentencing decisions.[34] In what follows, this Article summarizes the results of these bodies of research.

Race and the Administration of Capital Punishment in the United States

Numerous studies analyze whether race has impacted the (actual) administration of capital punishment in United States since its reinstatement by the Supreme Court in the late 1970s.[35] Importantly, most of these studies have been conducted in states that utilize capital punishment far more than Washington State.[36] Research shows that race continues to permeate the capital sentencing process despite the adoption of procedures designed to eliminate that possibility. This appears to have been the case in the years immediately following the Furman decision[37] and in more recent decades as well. However, while most studies focusing on the more recent period continue to find that the race of the victim influences capital outcomes, only about one-third of these studies find race-of-defendant effects.

A meta-analysis of studies published prior to 1990 conducted by the United States Government Accountability Office ("GAO") found "a pattern of evidence indicating racial disparities in the charging, sentencing and imposition of the death penalty after the Furman decision."[38] Studies published during this period consistently reported that defendants convicted of killing Whites were more likely to be sentenced to death than other defendants, over and above any differences in case characteristics.[39] Indeed, this finding was "remarkably consistent across data sets, states, data collection methods, and analytic techniques"; it was also found to exist at all stages of the criminal justice process.[40] Moreover, more than half of the studies reviewed by the GAO indicated that the race of the defendant also significantly impacted the likelihood that defendants were charged with a capital offense and sentenced to death prior to 1990. In three-fourths of these studies, Black defendants were significantly more likely to face a death sentence than similarly situated White defendants.[41]

More recent studies report similar findings.[42] In particular, studies analyzing more recent time periods fairly consistently report that victim-race and numerous other legal and extra-legal factors continue to influence the administration of capital punishment.[43] Specifically, most studies find that defendants convicted of killing Whites are significantly more likely to receive a death sentence than others, even after controlling for a wide range of legal and extra-legal factors that may also influence outcomes in capital cases.[44] For example, Songer and Unah analyzed capital sentencing in South Carolina in the 1990s and found that prosecutors were significantly more likely to seek death in cases involving White victims.[45] Similarly, Barnes, Sloss, and Thaman analyzed the imposition of the death penalty in cases adjudicated in Missouri between 1997 and 2001, and report that defendants accused of killing Whites were significantly more likely to be sentenced to death than other defendants after controlling for other relevant factors.[46] Radelet and Pierce analyzed the factors that predict the imposition of death sentences in eligible murder cases adjudicated in North Carolina between 1980 and 2007, and found that defendants accused of killing Whites were more likely to be sentenced to death than similarly situated others.[47] Numerous other studies have reached similar conclusions.[48]

Several recent studies also found that the race of the defendant influences outcomes in capital cases, with Black defendants more likely to be sentenced to death than similarly situated White defendants.[49] For example, Baldus reports that in cases adjudicated in Philadelphia between 1983 and 1993, Black defendants (and defendants accused of killing people who were not Black) were significantly more likely to be sentenced to death than similarly situated others.[50] Baldus similarly reports that Black defendants in the United States military system were more likely to be sentenced to death than non-Black defendants even after controlling for relevant legal factors.[51] Another recent study analyzing data from Arkansas found that Black defendants with White victims were significantly more likely to be sentenced to death than Black defendants with non-White victims and all White defendants.[52] Even more recently, Donohue found that in Connecticut, minority defendants accused of killing White victims were substantially more likely to be charged and sentenced to death than other similarly situated defendants.[53]

Many of these studies further suggest that race may matter the most at the sentencing phase of capital trials. For example, Baldus examined capital cases in Philadelphia and found that Black defendants were significantly more likely to be sentenced to death after controlling for a host of other relevant factors.[54] In fact, it is conceivable that the absence of race-of-defendant effects in some published studies is a consequence of the failure to analyze prosecutorial and jury decision-making processes separately.

Studies also indicate that other extra-legal factors influence the administration of capital punishment.[55] For example, some researchers have found that defendants convicted of killing women or children, and those who used a knife, are more likely to receive the ultimate sanction.[56] The type of location also appears to matter, with defendants sentenced in rural and suburban areas more likely to be sentenced to death than their urban counterparts.[57]

In sum, there is substantial evidence that race and other extra-legal factors have continued to impact capital sentencing processes in locales across the country: most studies report that the race of the victim has a significant impact on capital case outcomes, and some, though not all, find that the race of the defendant also influences the administration of capital punishment. Studies that analyze prosecutorial and jury decision-making separately often find that race matters most at the sentencing phase of the capital process.[58]

Evidence that race continues to matter in capital cases challenges the widespread belief that we are, in the post-Furman era, [59] "post-racial." Although overt, conscious, and intentional racism has diminished considerably in recent years, a number of studies show that both structural racism—racially unequal outcomes that flow from facially neutral institutional arrangements, policies or practices—and implicit (i.e., unconscious) racial bias persist.[60] Indeed, numerous experimental studies of implicit bias show that race affects perception and decision-making even in the absence of overt racial animus or antipathy.

[...]

Footnotes

1. The Death Penalty in 2013: Year End Report, Death Penalty Information Center, http://deathpenaltyinfo.org/documents/YearEnd2013.pdf.

2. See generally , CHARLES J. OGLETREE , JR . & AUSTIN SARAT , FROM LYNCH MOBS TO THE KILLING STATE : RACE AND THE DEATH PENALTY IN AMERICA (2006). Capital punishment is also controversial in Washington State. In 2014, Governor Jay Inslee expressed deep concerns about capital punishment and declared a moratorium on it. See Jennifer Sullivan & Andrew Garber, Inslee Halts Executions , SEATTLE TIMES (February 12, 2014), http://www.seattletimes.com/seattle-news/inslee-halts-executions-impact-on-current-cases-may-be-minimal/. In response, state prosecutors have asked lawmakers to introduce a referendum that will enable voters to determine the fate of capital punishment. See Associated Press, Washington Prosecutors Want Public Vote on Death Penalty, SEATTLE TIMES (November 13, 2015), http://www.seattletimes.com/seattle-news/crime/washington-prosecutors-want-death-penaltyreferendum/.

3. See, e.g. , James Liebman, Jeffrey Fagan & Valerie West, A Broken System: Error Rates in Capital Cases, 1973-1995 , http://www2.law.columbia.edu/instructionalservices/liebman/; Justin Marceau, Sam Kamin & Wanda Foglia, Death Eligibility in Colorado: Many are Called, Few are Chosen , 84 U. COLO . L. REV . 1069 (2013). Regarding pain and suffering, see Larry Greenemeier, Cruel and Unusual?: Is Capital Punishment by

Lethal Injection Quick and Painless?, SCIENTIFIC AMERICAN (October 27, 2010), http://www.scientificamerican.com/article/capital-punishment-by-lethal-injection/.

4. See, e.g. , American Civil Liberties Union, Race and the Death Penalty, https:// www.aclu.org/race-and-deathpenalty. See also , STUART BANNER , THE DEATH PENALTY : AN AMERICAN HISTORY (2009); Craig Haney, Condemning the Other in Death Penalty Trials: Biographical Racism, Structural Mitigation, and the Empathic Divide , 53 DE PAUL L. REV . 1557 (2004); Charles J. Ogletree, Jr., Black Man's Burden: Race and the Death Penalty in America , 81 OR . L. REV . 15, 18 (2002); Touré, Put to Death for Being Black: New Hope Against Judicial System Bias , TIME.com (May 03, 2012), http://ideas.time.com/2012/05/03/put-to-death-for-being-black-new-hope-against-judicial-system-bias/.

5. Stephen B. Bright, Discrimination, Death and Denial: The Tolerance of Racial Discrimination in the Infliction of the Death Penalty , 35 SANTA CLARA L. REV . 433, 433–34 (1995).

6. Furman v. Georgia, 408 U.S. 238 (1972). For an overview, see David C. Baldus & George Woodworth, Race Discrimination and the Death Penalty , in JAMES R. ACKER , ROBERT M. BOHM & CHARLES S. LANIER , AMERICA 'S EXPERIMENT WITH CAPITAL PUNISHMENT : REFLECTIONS ON THE PAST , PRESENT , AND FUTURE OF THE ULTIMATE PENAL SANCTION , 519–26 (2nd ed. 2003). See also , U.S. GOV 'T ACCOUNTABILITY OFF ., GGD-90-57, DEATH PENALTY SENTENCING : RESEARCH INDICATES PATTERN OF RACIAL DISPARITIES (1990); SAMUEL WALKER , CASSIA SPOHN & MIRIAM DE LONE , THE COLOR OF JUSTICE : RACE , ETHNICITY AND CRIME IN AMERICA (4th ed. 2006); JAMIE L. FLEXON , RACIAL DISPARITIES IN CAPITAL SENTENCING : PREJUDICE AND DISCRIMINATION IN THE JURY ROOM (2012).

7. See Baldus & Woodworth, supra note 6. See also U.S. GOV 'T ACCOUNTABILITY OFF ., U.S. GOV 'T ACCOUNTABILITY OFF ., supra note 6, at 5; WALKER , SPOHN & DE LONE , supra note 6; FLEXON , supra note 6.

8. U.S. GOV 'T ACCOUNTABILITY OFF ., supra note 6.

9. Lawrence Bobo, James R. Kluegel & Ryan A. Smith, Laissez-Faire Racism: The Crystallization of a 'Kinder, Gentler' Antiblack Ideology , in RACIAL ATTITUDES IN THE 1990S : CONTINUITY AND CHANGE (1997); Adam R. Pearson, John F. Dovidio & Samuel L. Gaertner, The Nature of Contemporary Prejudice: Insights from Aversive Racism , 3 SOC . & PERSONALITY PSYCHOL . COMPASS 314, 315 (2009).

10. Wash. Rev. Code § 10.95.030 (2015).

13. Marceau, Kamin & Foglia, supra note 3, at 1087.

14. See Kirchmeier, supra note 12.

15. See infra notes 67–69.

16. See SNELL , supra note 12.

17. Marceau, Kamin & Foglia, supra note 3.

18. This figure was calculated as follows: First, we obtained data regarding the number of aggravated and nonaggravated first-degree murder convictions from 1999-2013 from the Washington State Sentencing Guidelines Commission. See Statistical Summary of Adult Felony Sentencing, 1999-2013 , WASHINGTON STATE CASELOAD FORECAST COUNCIL , http://www.cfc.wa.gov/CriminalJustice_ADU_SEN.htm. We then subtracted the number of aggravated murder convictions involving non-

death eligible defendants from the total number of aggravated murder convictions. Defendants who were juveniles at the time of the conviction or subject to an extradition agreement that precluded the death penalty were considered ineligible for the death penalty. Finally, we calculated the percent of all first degree murder convictions that involved death-eligible defendants.

19. Death Row Inmates by State , DEATH PENALTY INFORMATION CENTER , http://www.deathpenaltyinfo.org/death-row-inmates-state-and-size-death-row-year (last updated Jan. 1, 2016).

20. Facts About the Death Penalty , DEATH PENALTY INFORMATION CENTER , http://www.deathpenaltyinfo.org/documents/FactSheet.pdf (last updated April 18, 2016).

21. Marceau, Kamin & Foglia, supra note 3, at 1094.

22. Furman v. Georgia, 408 U.S. 238 (1972).

23. Zant v. United States, 462 U.S. 862, 865 (1983). See also Marceau, Kamin & Foglia, supra note 3, at 1081–82 (discussing the narrowing of the class of persons eligible for the death penalty).

24. Marceau, Kamin & Foglia, supra note 3, at 1083.

25. See Sullivan & Garber, supra note 2. See Associated Press, supra note 2.

26. As of 2000, the federal courts had overturned seven of eight cases upheld by the Washington State Supreme Court. These cases included Mak v. Blodgett, 970 F.2d 614 (9th Cir. 1992), cert. denied , 507 U.S. 951 (1993); Harris by and through Ramseyer v. Blodgett, 853 F. Supp. 1239 (W. D. Wash. 1994), aff'd , 64 F.3d 1432 (9th Cir. 1995); Rupe v. Wood, 93 F.3d 1434 (9th Cir. 1996), cert. denied , 519 U.S. 1142 (1997); Jeffries v. Wood, 114 F.3d 1484 (9th Cir. 1997); Rice v. Wood, C89-568T (W.D. Wash. 1997); Lord v. Wood, 184 F.3d 1083 (9th Cir. 1999); Benn v. Wood, 2000 WL 1031361 (W.D. Wash. 2000). The one exception was Campbell v. Wood, 18 F.3d 662 (9th Cir. 1994) (en banc). See ACLU of Washington, Sentenced to Death: A Report on Washington Supreme Court Rulings in Capital Cases 2 (2000). Since 2000, federal courts have overturned one of three death sentences upheld by the Washington State Supreme Court. In 2002, the Ninth Circuit reversed the death sentence in Pirtle v. Morgan, 313 F.3d 1160 (9th Cir. 2002). In 2007, however, the United States Supreme Court affirmed Cal Brown's sentence. See Uttecht v. Brown, 551 U.S. 1 (2007). Jonathan Gentry also lost his federal appeal in the Ninth Circuit. See Gentry v. Sinclair, 705 F.3d 884 (9th Cir. 2012).

27. See, for example, the recent statement unanimously adopted by all nine Seattle councilmembers. Steve Militich, Seattle City Leaders Urge State Legislators to Abolish Death Penalty, SEATTLE TIMES (Jan. 26, 2015), http://blogs.seattletimes.com/today/2015/01/seattle-city-leaders-urge-state-legislators-to-abolish-death-penalty/. See also Mishi Faruqee, Facing Race and the Death Penalty , ACLU OF WASHINGTON BLOG (Dec. 11, 2012), https://acluwa.org/blog/facing-race-and-death-penalty.

28. Figures are current as of January 1, 2016, and are available through the Death Penalty Information Center. Current Death Row Populations by Race , DEATH PENALTY INFORMATION CENTER , http://www.deathpenaltyinfo.org/racedeath- row-inmates-executed-1976#deathrowpop (last updated Jan. 1, 2016).

31. See Ogletree, Jr., supra note 4. See also OGLETREE , JR . & SARAT , supra note 2.

32. See supra notes 7–8. See infra notes 49–56, 59, 66–69, 72.

33. See supra notes 7–8. See infra notes 49–56, 59.

34. See infra notes 66–69, 72.

35. Gregg v. Georgia, 428 U.S. 153 (1976).

36. See infra notes 50–65, 66–73.

37. Furman v. Georgia, 408 U.S. 238 (1972).

38. U.S. GOV 'T ACCOUNTABILITY OFF ., supra note 6, at 5.

39. U.S. GOV 'T ACCOUNTABILITY OFF ., supra note 6, at 5.

40. U.S. GOV 'T ACCOUNTABILITY OFF ., supra note 6, at 5.

41. U.S. GOV 'T ACCOUNTABILITY OFF ., supra note 6, at 6.

42. In a meta-analysis of the literature published in 2003, Baldus and Woodworth found that "in [eighty-three percent] (25/30) of the jurisdictions with relevant data, there is some evidence of race-of-victim disparities adversely affecting defendants whose victims are White, and in [thirty-three percent] (10/30) of these jurisdictions, there is some evidence of race-of-defendant disparities adversely affecting Black defendants." See Baldus & Woodworth, supra note 6, at 519.

43. See Baldus & Woodworth, supra note 6, at 519

44. See Baldus & Woodworth, supra note 6, at 520–21.

45. Michael J. Songer & Issac Unah, The Effect of Race, Gender and Location on Prosecutorial Decisions to Seek the Death Penalty in South Carolina , 58 S.C. L. REV . 161 (2006).

46. Katherine Y. Barnes, David L. Sloss & Stephen C. Thaman, Life and Death Decisions: Prosecutorial Discretion and Capital Punishment in Missouri 58 (Ariz. Legal Studies, Discussion Paper No. 08-03, 2008).

47. Michael L. Radelet & Glenn L. Pierce, Race and Death Sentencing in North Carolina, 1980-2007 , 89 N. C. L. REV . 2119, 2140–42 (2011).

48. See David C. Baldus, Catherine M. Grosso, George G. Woodworth & Richard Newell, Racial Discrimination in the Administration of the Death Penalty: The Experience of the United States Armed Forces (1984-2005) , 101 J. CRIM . L. & CRIMINOLOGY 1227 (2011); Glenn L. Pierce & Michael L. Radelet, Death Sentencing in East Baton Rouge Parish, 1990-2008 , 71 LA . L. REV 647 (2011); Glenn L. Pierce & Michael L. Radelet, The Impact of Legally Inappropriate Factors on Death Sentencing for California Homicides, 1990-1999 , 46 SANTA CLARA L. REV . 1 (2005); Scott Phillips, Continued Racial Disparities in the Capital of Capital Punishment: The Rosenthal Era , 50 HOUS . L. REV . 131 (2012).

49. Baldus & Woodworth, supra note 6, at 519.

50. David C. Baldus, George Woodworth, David Zuckerman, Neil A. Weiner & Barbara Broffitt, Racial Discrimination and the Death Penalty in the Post- Furman Era: An Empirical and Legal Overview, with Recent Findings from Philadelphia , 83 CORNELL L. REV . 1638 (1998).

51. Baldus, Grosso, Woodworth & Newell, supra note 50.

52. David C. Baldus, Julie Brain, Neil A. Weiner & George Woodworth, Evidence of Racial Discrimination in the Use of the Death Penalty: A Story from Southwest Arkansas (1990-2005) with Special Reference to the Case of Death Row Inmate Frank Williams, Jr. , 76 TENN . L. REV . 555 (2009).

53. John J. Donohue III, An Empirical Evaluation of the Connecticut Death Penalty System since 1973: Are there Unlawful Racial, Gender and Geographic Disparities? , Stanford Law School, Working Paper No. 464 (2014), http://ssrn.com/abstract=2470082.

54. Baldus, Woodworth, Zuckerman, Weiner & Broffitt, supra note 51, at 1714.

55. Donohue III, supra note 53, at 696.

56. See Songer & Unah, supra note 45, at 191–97.

57. See Baldus & Woodworth, supra note 6, at 520; Donohue III, supra note 53, at 52–57.

58. Baldus, Woodworth, Zuckerman, Weiner & Broffitt, supra note 50, at 1715–22; Isaac Unah, Empirical Analysis of Race and the Process of Capital Punishment in North Carolina , 2011 MICH . ST . L. REV . 609, 646–48 (2011).

59. Furman v. Georgia, 408 U.S. 238 (1972).

60. Bobo, Kluegel & Smith, supra note 9.

7

How Gender Affects the Death Penalty

Amanda Oliver

Amanda Oliver works as an executive director of a non-profit and also blogs on The Color Coded Life. *She is a proud supporter of women's and reproductive rights, civil rights, and LGBTQ+ rights.*

Though she was executed in 1998, a Georgia woman's fate at the hands of the law still brings to the forefront questions about a gender bias in the death penalty. Women appear differently to a jury, mostly as nonthreatening, unless they are presented as promiscuous. There is also the idea that men are more likely to kill than women. That Kelly Gissendaner was the first woman executed in Georgia in 70 years while approximately 1400 men had been executed across the country during that same time only seems to support the assertion that the death penalty is disproportionately stacked against male perpetrators of violent crime.

At 12:21 a.m. ET on Wednesday, September 30, Kelly Gissendaner became the 16th woman executed in the United States since the U.S. Supreme Court reinstated the death penalty in 1976. The Georgia woman was sentenced to death in 1998 for convincing her boyfriend to shoot her husband and was the first woman in 70 years to be executed in that state. However, in these same 39 years, the United States has executed 1,399 men. Even death row shows a gender bias, where of the 3,035 people on death

"The Death Penalty Has a Gender Bias," by Amanda Oliver, The Huffington Post, October 1, 2016. Reprinted by Permission.

row, only 54 of them are women. Why is it so rare for a woman to be put to death?

A quick background on the death penalty would include the fact that there are 31 states that still provide this punishment. However, the South tends to use the punishment more frequently, with Texas and Oklahoma alone accounting for 640 of the 1,415 executions since 1976. On average, women account for 10 percent of the arrests for murder. However, as the legal process moves towards death row, the percentage of women decreases significantly. Only 1.1 percent of women are eventually executed, including the execution this week of Gissendaner. So what accounts for this drastic difference in the number of women executed?

Let's break down the main arguments:

Argument #1: Women Commit Fewer Murders Than Men

One argument is that men commit more murders and death penalty-worthy crimes than women. The numbers back this theory, with men at fault for 90 percent of the 15,094 murders committed in 2010 (the most recent year for which the FBI has data). What the numbers do not take into account is the fact that not all murders are considered eligible to face the death penalty. Additionally, how the murder was committed (not to get too graphic) also plays a role in sentencing. The factors that go into how a person gets the death penalty tends to favor women (which I will explain more below).

Even with these numbers, this argument is flawed. When the statistics are adjusted for the larger number of murders by men, women are still sentenced to death at a lower rate.

Argument #2: We Live in A Chivalrous Society

With the fact that we still need feminism to gain basic equality in the United States, there's no question that we still live in a very paternalistic society. But is this belief that men need to "protect" women impacting whether they receive the death penalty?

Death Penalty Information Center Executive Director Richard Dieter told *Business Insider* that it's as simple as the fact that, when it comes to murderers, "'[j]urors just see women differently than men.'"

It's often the idea that women were acting under the influence of others or are emotionally fragile, and therefore shouldn't be held as accountable as men. *Business Insider* quotes Ohio Northern University Law Professor Victor Streib as saying, "'It's just easier to convince a jury that women suffer from emotional distress or other emotional problems more than men.'"

This belief of the sad, weak woman leads into the third argument as to why so few women receive the death penalty.

Argument #3: The Evil Woman Theory

According to some researchers, it's only the women who fall into certain categories that "gain" the protection from chivalry. The women who benefit are the feminine, docile, mothering, and chaste women (also, likely white and heterosexual). It is the un-ladylike, aggressive, or sexually promiscuous women who jurors see as more of a "threat" to society.

Gissendaner is a perfect example of this theory in action. She falls under the "un-ladylike" and "sexually promiscuous" umbrella, since she was having an affair and had her then-boyfriend kill her husband.

While the second two arguments may not be as false as the first one, they still don't fully explain why so few women are ever put to death. The main reason is much less interesting, but all the more important.

Argument #4: Men are sentenced to death more than women because of how the statutes are written and how the circumstances around the crimes are weighed.

I know, boring, right?

But think about it—who was eligible to be elected to state legislatures for most of our country's history? Old (mostly white) men.

Therefore, who likely wrote the statutes for murder? Old, white men.

Who decided which factors would favor someone getting the death penalty (called "aggravating factors") and which would count towards them not getting it (called "mitigating factors")? Old, white men.

So, it makes sense that the statutes are written with the male belief as to what crimes are worse and when factors should point towards the death penalty.

Although the list of specific factors can vary by state, most states include as aggravating factors the potential future dangerousness of a defendant, their prior history of violence, whether the murder was during the commission of another felony, and their criminal record. Common mitigating factors can include whether the defendant was under extreme emotional or mental disturbance, whether they were under the control of someone else, their "good" character, and their family background. Since previous histories of violence and criminal records play heavily in favor of getting the death penalty, these factors also favor women. Women murderers generally do not have much (if any) history of violence or criminal records.

Most states that still practice capital punishment also do not have the killing of an intimate partner or a child as an aggravating favor. Yet, these are exactly the types of murders that women are most likely to commit according to Professor Elizabeth Rappaport of the University of New Mexico Law School. According to a study by the NIH, 60 percent of the murders committed by women were against a family member or intimate partner, compared with only 20 percent of men. Look again at the case that started this article—Kelly Gissendaner had her then-boyfriend kill her husband.

It seems that men find the idea of killing a stranger more horrific (or at least an affront to their manhood) than the thought of killing someone they know. In 80 percent of the murders committed by men, their victims were either strangers or someone they barely knew. A study conducted in South Carolina found that murders committed against strangers were six times more likely to get the death penalty. This lends support to the theory that murders against strangers tend to favor men receiving the death penalty.

Further supporting this is the research that found that the types of murders that most often receive the death penalty (murder for gain, murder while resisting law enforcement or an especially cruel murder), do not include murdering someone the person knew or lived with.

The truth behind why so many women are not executed may not be terribly "sexy" or interesting, but it is still important. The United States is one of only a small number of nations that continues to practice the death penalty. Even worse, the *Washington Post* reported that the United States has five more executions over the next week. With all of this, plus the Pope's recent visit and remarks against the death penalty, now is the time to take a stand against capital punishment.

8

Misrepresentation in Capital Cases

Capital Punishment in Context

Capital Punishment in Context explores the cases of several individuals who were given the death penalty in the United States in order to contextualize capital punishment and open up further discussion on these issues..

The Constitution grants everyone facing trial the right to an attorney and fair treatment under the law. However, the idea of fairness gets warped as many defendants are unable to afford good lawyers and a proper defense. These mitigating factors can lead to errors in trial and unfortunate decisions being made. Some of these consequences are illustrated through high-profile death penalty cases—including that of serial killer Aileen Wuornos, who was the subject of both a documentary and a 2003 Hollywood film.

Defense Representation in Capital Cases

The Constitution guarantees a criminal defendant a right to an attorney and to due process of law. The Supreme Court has held that legal counsel must provide effective representation. Almost all defendants in capital cases cannot afford their own attorneys. In many cases the appointed attorneys are overworked, underpaid, or lacking the trial experience required for death penalty cases. Because the American system of criminal justice is adversarial, depending upon contesting presentations by capable lawyers for the prosecution and the defense to arrive at fair and accurate results, it is essential that defense counsel be sufficiently skilled and experienced and be given adequate resources to fulfill his or her obligations to the client and the court.

Assessing the Importance of Quality Representation in Capital Cases

The Supreme Court, the Department of Justice and the American Bar Association are just some of the organizations involved in defining what constitutes adequate representation in capital cases. The following supplementary materials can help you further investigate this issue.

Key Supreme Court Cases on Capital Representation

Supreme Court decisions addressing representation fall into two major categories: those that define the parameters of the right to counsel and those that discuss standards for counsel's performance. Each of these categories is important in the discussion of capital defense practices.

Right to Counsel for Indigent Criminal Defendants

Even though the right to counsel in criminal proceedings is guaranteed by the Sixth Amendment, this right only protected criminal defendants in federal prosecutions until two cases extended the protection to individuals prosecuted by state governments. *Powell v. Alabama* (1932) secured the right to an attorney for indigent capital defendants, and *Gideon v. Wainwright* (1963) extended that right to all indigent criminal defendants at the trial level. In *Douglas v. California* (1963), the Court held that when a state affords a defendant a right to appeal, it must provide an attorney to indigent defendants for the first statutory appeal. This appeal, which concerns matters that arose during the trial, is called the "direct appeal." Subsequent review is referred to as "post-conviction proceedings." In *Murray v. Giarratano* (1989) the Court refused to find, at least where capital defendants were receiving some legal assistance for post-conviction proceedings, that there was a constitutional right to representation in such matters.

Evaluating the Effectiveness of Counsel

After the right to counsel was established, the Supreme Court issued a series of decisions that evaluated the effectiveness of trial counsel. *Strickland v. Washington* (1984) established a framework for evaluating attorney performance in capital cases. Strickland requires that the defendant prove that counsel's representation was deficient and that there is a reasonable probability that, but for counsel›s deficiency, the outcome of the trial would have been different. Ineffective assistance of counsel is established only when the defendant has satisfied BOTH prongs of the Strickland test. In making determinations about what constitutes deficient representation, the Court has recently focused on the extent to which capital defense counsel investigate potential mitigating evidence on behalf of their clients. In *Williams v. Taylor* (2000) and *Wiggins v. Smith* (2003), the Court ruled that failure to conduct a thorough investigation of the client's background may constitute ineffective assistance of counsel. The court further defined defense counsel's obligation to investigate in *Rompilla v. Beard* (2005), which held that even when a capital defendant and his family members have suggested that no mitigating evidence is available, his lawyer is bound to make reasonable efforts to obtain and review material that counsel knows the prosecution will probably rely on as evidence of aggravation at the trial's sentencing phase.

Standards for Counsel in Capital Cases

Strickland provided the framework under which courts evaluate claims of ineffective assistance of counsel, but the Court has not specifically defined a set of performance standards for capital defense attorneys. Both the Department of Justice and the American Bar Association have published criteria to be used in evaluating trial counsel.

Representation Issues in the Gary Graham Case

The case of Gary Graham highlights some of the legal hurdles that capital defendants face. For example, because Texas had no state public defender system when Graham was tried (and still does not have one), each county was responsible for guaranteeing that the constitutional right to counsel was honored when poor people faced criminal charges. Most counties, including Harris County, where Graham was tried, appointed private attorneys to provide indigent defense. Counsel were paid very little: at the time of Graham's trial, attorneys representing capital clients were paid on average less than $50 an hour for in-court time and nothing for out-of-court time.

Graham's legal challenge to this process was filed with the U.S. Department of Justice by the NAACP Legal Defense Fund just days before his first scheduled execution date. The complaint asserted that this practice created a system where attorneys' economic interests were in fundamental conflict with their clients' interests. Graham claimed that the inadequacies of Texas' indigent defense system made it extremely unlikely that any lawyer appointed to a capital case would be able to provide effective assistance.

According to Graham, the Texas compensation scheme created an incentive for attorneys to forgo the out-of-court preparation necessary to develop a good in-court case and encouraged lawyers to "wing it" in court. For example, attorneys wanting to increase their in-court compensation might conduct long in-court examinations of witnesses whom they had never previously interviewed, thereby failing to bring out useful information, and instead, bring out information damaging to their clients. Graham requested that the Department of Justice conduct a full investigation into the systematic deprivations of constitutional rights outlined in the complaint, and that it initiate appropriate legal actions to enforce compliance with the Constitution.

Beyond systemic issues concerning capital representation in Texas, Graham claimed that his trial counsel, Ron Mock, had failed to adequately defend him and that Mock's representation was so ineffective as to call the outcome of the trial into question. Graham asserted that defense counsel was ineffective for failing to conduct a thorough investigation and to present all of the relevant evidence. Ultimately, Graham argued, "defense counsel, through a combination of mistakes, misunderstandings, confusions, and omissions, failed to provide Mr. Graham the 'zealous defense' upon which the integrity of the criminal justice system relies."

According to Graham, his trial counsel's performance was deficient in several areas:

- He failed to investigate Graham's account of his whereabouts on the night of the murder;
- He failed to investigate adequately the reliability of witnesses identifying Graham as the perpetrator; and
- He failed to call defense witnesses at trial.

To rebut Graham's claims of ineffective assistance of counsel, the State presented evidence, including affidavits by Ron Mock, that Mock did as good a job of defending Graham as could have been done under the circumstances of Graham's case. Specifically, the state argued that on numerous occasions prior to trial, Mock met with Graham and attempted to discuss the facts of the case with him. Graham only stated that he did not commit the robbery-murder and that he spent the evening with a girlfriend whose name, appearance, and address he could not remember. The state further contended that despite defense counsel's effort, Graham did not provide the names of any potential alibi witnesses nor did he reveal where he had been or what he had been doing on the night of the homicide. Furthermore, the defense hired an investigator, Merv West, who interviewed at least ten potential mitigation witnesses. Only two, his stepfather and grandmother, would agree to testify favorably at trial. The state also asserted that Mock informed Graham that he had a right to testify on his own behalf but Graham never told trial counsel that he wanted to testify at either the guilt/innocence or punishment phases of the trial.

All of Graham's claims of ineffective representation were rejected by the appellate courts.

Questions for Further Analysis

- How could poor-quality of representation increase the likelihood of wrongful convictions in capital cases? How could it increase the likelihood that a convicted defendant would be sentenced to death when, with a more capable attorney, he or she might have received a less severe punishment?
- Should death sentenced inmates be guaranteed the right to an attorney in post-conviction proceedings?
- Should there be national standards for attorneys in capital cases? Who should set these standards? Should these requirements apply to both the defense and the prosecution?
- Do the Supreme Court's decisions in the Williams, Wiggins and Rompilla cases seem to demand more in the way of investigation by a capital defendant's lawyer than was demanded by the Supreme Court's earlier decisions such as *Strickland v. Washington*? If so, would this higher standard of duty apply to the defendant's lawyer at the guilt/innocence stage of a capital trial, as well as to the sentencing stage with which the Williams, Wiggins and Rompilla cases were specifically concerned? If the standard for counsel's performance established by the Supreme Court's cases since 2000 had been in effect at the time when Gary Graham's claim of ineffective assistance of counsel was presented to the courts, would the courts' rulings on that claim have been different?

Representation Issues in the Anthony Porter Case

The Anthony Porter case highlights the significant impact ineffective assistance of counsel can have on the outcome of capital cases. Even before the trial started, the odds were against Porter. Akim Gursel, who became Porter's primary lawyer, had had earlier unfavorable encounters with the judge who was presiding over Porter's trial. After calling only three witnesses during the guilt phase, Gursel opted for judge sentencing because Porter's family had been unable to pay his attorney fees and a judge sentencing would be less work than a jury sentencing.

During his post-conviction appeals, Porter's appellate attorneys twice raised the issue of ineffective assistance of counsel. As with any such claim, Porter needed to prove that his counsel's performance was below an objective standard of reasonableness and that a "reasonable probability" existed that, but for counsel's deficienies, the result of the proceeding would have been different. (*Strickland v. Washington*—will link to case)

In his 1995 petition for post-conviction relief, Porter contended that he was entitled to a new trial because his attorney did not present evidence showing that Alstory Simon, rather than Porter, killed Hillard and Green. Porter pointed to the testimony of two witnesses who would have revealed that the victims walked to the park with Simon and his girlfriend, Inez Jackson, and that Simon had been in a dispute with Hillard regarding drug money. Porter argued that his attorney did not call these witnesses during his trial because he (Porter) was unable to pay the remainder of the fees owed to the attorney. Gursel admitted that he stopped investigating the case because Porter was able to pay him only $3,000 of the $10,000 fee previously agreed upon.

In denying post-conviction relief, the Illinois Supreme Court held that even if Porter's trial attorney performed ineffectively by not presenting these witnesses, there was no reasonable likelihood of a different outcome. The court said there was considerable evidence against Porter that was unaffected by the trial attorney's error, namely testimony by Henry Williams, William Taylor and Officer Anthony Liance.

The issue of ineffective assistance of counsel was addressed again in Porter's 1997 petition to the federal courts for a writ of habeas corpus. His federal habeas lawyers argued to the United States Court of Appeals for the Seventh Circuit that:

- Counsel failed to pursue evidence suggesting that someone other than Porter was the murderer;
- Counsel failed to fully investigate Porter's alibi defense;

- Counsel failed to prepare two alibi witnesses that were called at trial; and
- Counsel failed to meet with Porter except immediately before and after court proceedings.

The Court of Appeals denied Porter's petition, despite taking all of his allegations to be true. It reasoned that Porter could not demonstrate that better representation would probably have resulted in an acquittal. According to the court, "the affidavits and statements that Porter has submitted are far from convincing, especially when weighed against the direct, eyewitness testimony implicating Porter."

Porter's case highlights a potential problem in post-conviction proceedings based on claims of ineffective assistance of counsel that will be discussed at greater length in a separate essay, but is worth a brief mention here. According to Strickland, judges in post-conviction proceedings must be convinced both that the trial lawyer's performance was ineffective and that there is a reasonable likelihood that the outcome of the trial would have been different if the lawyer had been competent. According to these standards, the defendant is not entitled to a new trial even if his lawyer failed to present evidence of innocence during the trial unless the post-conviction judges also find that this evidence would have led the jury to acquit the defendant. Most claims of ineffective assistance of counsel are turned down by the courts on this account, and not because the lawyers are found to have performed competently.

In Porter's case, both the state courts and federal courts concluded that there was no reasonable likelihood that Porter could be found innocent, yet a thorough investigation later conducted by journalism students ultimately revealed that Porter actually was innocent, and the real killer confessed to the crime for which Porter had been wrongly convicted.

Questions for Further Analysis

- Can the risk of executing the innocent be completely eliminated? If so, how can this be done?

- If not, can the risk be substantially reduced? How can this be done? What costs would be involved in changing the system of trials and appeals and postconviction proceedings so as to substantially reduce the risks? Would the reduction of the risk be worth these costs?
- Should convictions or sentences be overturned if the attorney was ineffective, even though the court doesn't believe the outcome would likely have been different?
- Porter's case also raises questions about the special problems that individuals with intellectual disabilities may face when they are charged with a crime and required to defend themselves in court. [See Intellectual Disabilities and the Death Penalty] Is there any connection between these problems and the problem of assuring that these defendants receive effective legal representation?

Representation Issues in the Aileen Wuornos Case

Aileen Wuornos' appeals raised the issue of inadequate representation in her trial for the murder of Richard Mallory, as well as in her other five cases (the murders of David Spears, Charles Carskaddon, Tony Burress, Charles Humphreys, and Walter Antonio), for which she pled guilty or no contest. In her appeal to the Florida Supreme Court, Wuornos contended that her penalty phase lawyer in the Mallory case failed to call as mitigation witnesses people who had known her as a child and who would have humanized her by describing the abuse she experienced. The court held that her counsel was not ineffective because much of the information offered by those witnesses was presented to the jury by three defense experts who testified during the penalty phase.

In addition, Wuornos claimed inadequate representation because her defense counsel had not uncovered evidence of Mallory's past criminal conviction, which could have corroborated her argument that she committed the murder in self-defense. The court rejected this claim because such evidence is admissible only under two conditions: the first is "to present the general reputation for violence the victim has in the community" and the second is to allow "evidence of the specific violent acts of the victim if known to the defendant." In responding to Wuornos' appeal, the Florida Supreme Court stated that "The defendant does not claim that she was aware of Mr. Mallory's criminal past at the time of his murder. Consequently, the fact that Mr. Mallory was charged with a sex offense well over thirty years prior to his fatal encounter with Wuornos is not relevant."

Wuornos hired a new lawyer, Steven Glazer. Glazer entered a "no contest" plea for the murders of Dick Humphreys, Troy Burress, and David Spears on the same day as he filed notice that he was taking her case. Wuornos' appeal in the Walter Antonio case, in which she originally pled guilty, argues that Glazer "professed a lack of experience needed to represent her during a guilt-phase trial and, as a result, had an inherent conflict of interest when permitting her to enter a guilty plea." She also argued that her plea was not voluntary because Glazer did not advise her of its consequences.

Tricia Jenkins, Wuornos' original attorney, later testified that Glazer had not picked up discovery files from her regarding Wuornos' case, and that "he told me he was taking the case because he needed the media exposure." In her appeal of the Charles Carskaddon case, in which Glazer filed Wuornos' guilty plea, Wuornos claimed a conflict of interest between herself and Glazer, based on movie and book deals Glazer had sought. Additional problems with Glazer's representation were raised in the documentary "Aileen: Life and Death of a Serial Killer" by Nick Bloomfield, in which Glazer requests payment of $25,000 for an interview, stating that Wuornos was unable to pay him and he needed the interview payment to work on her case.

In 2001, Wuornos dropped her appeals. Numerous attorneys, advocacy groups, and mental health experts appealed to have the courts allow them to act on her behalf, arguing that her deteriorating mental state made her incompetent to waive her appeals or to be executed. Following a 30-minute psychiatric assessment of

Wuornos by three of Governor Jeb Bush's handpicked experts, the courts concluded that she was competent and allowed her death warrant to stand.

Although Wuornos' case raises a number of other issues, problems with her representation were the main focus of her appeals. Similar problems have arisen in other capital cases in which overworked public defenders cannot give cases the attention they need. Additionally, Glazer's quest for publicity highlights the particular dangers in highly publicized cases and illustrates the influence of the media in such cases.

Questions for Further Analysis

- What specific disadvantages would an inexperienced lawyer face in arguing a complex capital case?
- How might the influence of the media in a high-profile case affect a lawyer's ability to represent a client adequately? What corrective actions can be taken?
- If an attorney stands to profit from a case, such as through book or movie deals, does that create a conflict of interest between the attorney and the client?
- If you were designing a legal criterion for deciding whether and attorney's performance was incompetent, what would it be?

9

How State Ordered Executions Challenge Medical Ethics

James K. Boehnlein

James K. Boehnlein, MD, is a professor of psychiatry at Oregon Health and Science University and director of medical student education for OHSU's Department of Psychiatry. He is also the associate director for education at the VA Northwest Network Mental Illness Research, Education, and Clinical Center (MIRECC) in Portland.

Physician participation is a vital part of carrying out the death penalty because of their skills and knowledge when it comes to administering a lethal injection. Without a competent medical professional on hand to monitor proceedings, an execution can go horribly wrong. Controversy arises as physicians are effectively aiding in taking a life—not sustaining it, like their oath requires them to, and it is often up to individual doctors whether to follow their personal philosophy, the American Medical Association's code of ethics, or the law of the state in which they practice.

Physician involvement in state-ordered executions has emerged as a controversial issue in medical ethics in the United States over the past couple of decades, due primarily to the increased, and now virtually exclusive, use of lethal injection for capital punishment. Although executions over centuries have employed

"Should Physicians Participate in State-Ordered Executions?" by James K. Boehnlein, American Medical Association, March 2013, Volume 15, Number 3: 240-243.

firing squads, hanging, electrocution, and gas asphyxiation, lethal injection is now the sole method of execution accepted by courts as humane enough to satisfy Eighth Amendment prohibitions against cruel and inhuman punishment, as confirmed by the Supreme Court in *Baze v. Rees.*[1]

Physician participation is central to execution by lethal injection because medical knowledge and skills are integral to conducting the procedure effectively. This means, however, that medical technology and physician expertise are utilized to end life rather than to sustain it. Those who believe that there should be medical participation in lethal injection argue that, since executions are a legal way for society to carry out retributive justice for those who have been convicted of heinous crimes, and since the execution will occur anyway, the participation of medical personnel is essential to minimize the suffering of the condemned prisoner.

If not done properly, the sequential use of sodium thiopental for anesthesia, pancuronium bromide for paralysis, and potassium chloride to cause cardiac arrest can go awry at any stage. For example, before the 2008 U.S. Supreme Court ruling upholding the constitutionality of capital punishment by lethal injection, a number of prisoners executed in California had not stopped breathing before technicians had given the paralytic agent, raising the possibility that they had experienced suffocation from the paralytic and felt intense pain from the potassium bolus.[2] Following a number of these botched executions, physicians and other health care professionals have increasingly been sought to provide consultation, place intravenous lines, mix and administer drugs, and monitor results.[3] But even evaluation of lethal injection drugs and procedures by various states has been problematic because none of the drug protocols were ever tested in animals before they were employed, and ongoing evaluation of drug protocols and devices resembles human subjects research, but without the usual established protections.[4]

Those who are opposed to physician participation in lethal injection argue that it is unethical on several counts: physician skills and procedures that contradict established medical practice are being used to carry out government mandates; a previously nonmedical social and judicial act is being medicalized; executions by lethal injection are carried out in a quasimedical setting and give the impression that a medical procedure is being administered[5]; and the doctor is using knowledge and skills attained during medical education and is recognized by society as possessing and using those specific skills that are normally used to sustain and enhance life.[6]

Those who argue for the validity of physician participation point out that professional medical organizations should not interfere with a doctor's personal beliefs about the suitability of capital punishment.[7] They refer here to the American Medical Association's (AMA) *Code of Medical Ethics*, which states that an individual's opinion on capital punishment is his or her personal moral decision but that "a physician, as a member of a profession dedicated to preserving life when there is hope of doing so, should not be a participant in a legally authorized execution."[8] In other words, a physician, just like any other individual in society, is entitled to his or her own opinion on specific ethical issues, but when he or she is utilizing medical knowledge or skills as a physician in any social realm, professional ethical standards should apply. To put it in stark terms, as Truog does, this would not prohibit physicians from participating in a firing squad (in their role as citizens), but it would prohibit their participation in lethal injections (in their role as physicians).[9]

An argument is sometimes raised that these professional standards may not apply to lethal injection because there is no established doctor-patient relationship. But the lack of such a relationship does not lessen the doctor's responsibility; even though a therapeutic relationship does not exist, the physician is still using medical knowledge and skills and still viewed by the corrections system, the state, and as society as functioning in a medical role. In addition, the condemned prisoner is not in a position to consent to or refuse what would normally be a medical procedure conducted by a physician (insertion of an IV and injection of drugs).

This leads to another important point of argument and discussion. Those who argue for a more permissive role for physicians in lethal injection assert that professional norms are not exclusively internal to the profession of medicine, but must be negotiated with society at large.[7] They point to the diversity of attitudes within the profession towards physician participation in assisted suicide and abortion, despite prohibition of the former by national professional organizations, as evidence of a more fluid interface between professional and social ethical norms. These proponents of physician choice on participation have a strong argument regarding the apparent inconsistency between professional standards that sometimes view physician-assisted suicide favorably[10] and physician participation in lethal injection unfavorably. However, their permissive argument breaks down in the context of consent—in lethal injection there is no consent by the condemned prisoner and there is no doctor-patient relationship as there is in physician-assisted suicide.

So a number of ethical issues make physician participation in lethal injection problematic. These include the medicalization of what is essentially a civil and legal procedure related to retributive justice and undertaken primarily to serve the goals of the state.[9] The fact that there is no patient-physician relationship and no consent to treatment actually supports the argument against participation rather than the one in favor of it. Even if there were a physician-patient relationship, which there is not, the result of an execution clearly harms the executed person without offsetting benefit.[11] Even though proponents of execution by lethal injection argue that it causes the condemned prisoner less suffering than other methods of execution[2], the end result is still the irrevocable death of the condemned prisoner. Furthermore, it is not the responsibility of medicine to ensure that executions take place—the use of and method for capital punishment are political and legal questions.[12]

A coherent and internally consistent set of norms for ethical conduct for physicians can be constructed based upon the goals of medicine, and these norms (drawn for centuries from widely accepted sources such as the Hippocratic Oath, which specifically states "I will not give a lethal drug to anyone if I am asked, nor will I advise such a plan" [13]) prohibit the involvement of physicians in state-sponsored killing.[9] Today that tradition includes the stance that it is immoral to develop humane methods to kill people legally.[14]

Professional values in medicine evolve in dynamic interaction with social norms. But defining one's professional role exclusively by societal norms diminishes individual professional responsibility to appropriately use the knowledge and skills of healing that are attained during medical education and training[6]. The physician needs to be cognizant of how his or her role is viewed by society in any given era and at the same time be able to clearly understand how the profession of medicine has developed and defined appropriate professional norms regarding physician behavior in actions related to life and death. This awareness must begin early in medical education and continue throughout professional life. This examination is not an easy task but it is essential to maintain individual and collective professional integrity in complex social situations that involve medical ethics.

References

1. *Baze v. Rees*, 553 US 35 (2008). http://supreme.justia.com/cases/federal/us/553/07-5439/. Accessed November 17, 2012.

2. Gawande A. When law and ethics collide—why physicians participate in executions. N Engl J Med. 2006;354(12):1221-1229.

3. Curfman GD, Morrissey S, Drazen JM. Physicians and execution. *N Engl J Med*. 2008;358(4):403-404.

4. Koniaris LG, Goodman KW, Sugarman J, Ozomaro U, Sheldon J, Zimmers TA. Ethical implications of modifying lethal injection protocols. *PLoS Med.* 2008;5(6):e126.

5. Trent B. Capital punishment: MD politicians share their views. *CMAJ.* 1986;143(7):792-798.

6. Boehnlein JK, Parker RM, Arnold RM, Bosk CF, Sparr LF. Medical ethics, cultural values, and physician participation in lethal injection. *Bull Am Acad Psychiatry Law.* 1995;23(1):129-134.

7. Nelson L, Ashby B. Rethinking the ethics of physician participation in lethal injection execution. *Hastings Cent Rep.* 2011;41(3):28-37.

8. American Medical Association. Opinion 2.06—capital punishment. *Code of Medical Ethics.* http://www.ama-assn.org/ama/pub/physician-resources/ medical-ethics/code-medical-ethics/opinion206.page. Accessed November 8, 2012.

9. Truog RD. Are there some things doctors just shouldn't do? *Hastings Cent Rep.* 2011;41(3);3.

10. Boehnlein JK. The case against physician assisted suicide. *Community Ment Health J.* 1999;35(1):5-14.

11. Black L, Sade RM. Lethal injection and physicians. *JAMA.* 2007;298(23):2779-2781.

12. Black L, Fairbrother H. The ethics of the elephant: why physician participation in executions remains unethical. *Am J Bioeth.* 2008;8(10):59-61.

13. National Institutes of Health. Greek medicine: "I swear by Apollo physician...": Greek medicine from the gods to Galen. http://www.nlm.nih.gov/hmd/greek/greek_oath.html. Accessed February 15, 2013.

14. Bewley T. A modest proposal for the medical profession to introduce humane and civilized executions. *J R Soc Med.* 2009;102(9):365-368.

10

Lethal Injections and the Law

Soli Salgado

Soli Salgado is a staff writer for Global Sisters Report, often covering issues related to the Hispanic community. She joined the National Catholic Reporter team as a Bertelsen intern in 2015 and has received several Catholic Press Awards.

The 2015 Supreme Court ruling to uphold lethal injections for the death penalty continues to stir up conversation. Proponents argued for a need to keep the method constitutional, and this was the best option. However, opponents of the death penalty—such as the Catholic Church—insist that the Supreme Court reconsider the decision, asking if the punishment can be stomached. If not, then the practice should be abolished. There is no humane way to put someone to death, some detractors point out. Meanwhile, others ask the vital question: Why shouldn't the punishment fit the crime?

As the Supreme Court upheld that the current procedure for lethal injection is constitutional in a 5-4 decision, Catholics, attorneys, and both proponents and opponents of the death penalty weighed in on the outcome of *Glossip* v. *Gross*.

The case, which tackled an unusually technical discussion on pharmaceutical options, ruled that Oklahoma's use of midazolam was not a form of cruel and unusual punishment when administered

"Supreme Court decision adds to ongoing debate about lethal injection," by Soli Salgado, National Catholic Reporter, July 1, 2015. Reprinted by Permission of National Catholic Reporter Publishing Company, 115E. Armour Blvd, Kansas City, MO 64111, Ncronline.org.

as the first of three drugs in the lethal cocktail, despite being a sedative rather than anesthetic.

But those on both sides of the debate—including the Supreme Court justices in both the majority opinion and dissent—agreed that this case transcended that specific issue indirectly.

Capital punishment is constitutional; therefore, there must be a constitutional way of carrying it out, Justice Samuel Alito wrote. Alito and proponents of the death penalty said challenging the use of midazolam was a tactic in unraveling the legality of the death penalty. While Justice Stephen Breyer's dissent—joined by Justice Ruth Bader Ginsburg—leaned toward its abolition, the majority maintained its lawfulness.

The Catholic church denounces capital punishment when other methods that respect human dignity are available to protect society, with sec. 2267 of the Catechism of the Catholic Church adding that cases where death is the appropriate response "are very rare, if not practically nonexistent." And Pope Francis has gone so far as to call for an end to life sentences.

"It's hard to imagine what could be crueler than a prolonged, torturous death, or more unusual, given that 80% of the executions in the United States last year took place in just 3 states," the National Coalition to Abolish the Death Penalty wrote in a statement following the ruling.

Opponents of the death penalty told *NCR* that how cruel and unusual this form of punishment is highlights the moral question: Can we find valid, ethical comfort in administering painless executions?

"We need to be clear that there is no humane way to put a person to death," said Alex Mikulich, a Catholic theologian at the Jesuit Social Research Institute at Loyola University New Orleans. "[Lethal injection] violates basic human dignity, and by imposing that kind of torture, it diminishes all of us. It dehumanizes us."

"I think people of faith who are against the death penalty— we're at a point where we need to redouble our efforts to end this practice in our country," he continued. "We clearly cannot rely on the courts to end it."

The *Glossip v. Gross* decision fell on the anniversary of *Furman v. Georgia*, the 1972 case that first ruled capital punishment as unconstitutional; however, the court then suggested legislation that would make death sentences constitutional again, such as standardized guidelines for juries. This makes the United States one of nine nations that Amnesty International lists as "persistent executioners," joined by China, Iraq, Iran, Saudi Arabia, Yemen, Sudan, Bangladesh and North Korea.

Under public pressure, European pharmaceutical companies that had provided states with the lethal drugs have stopped selling them for executions, forcing states to turn to alternates with unproven efficacy.

"The one thing that [this case] does show on the political side is that the campaign to make these drugs inaccessible has worked," said David Burge, an attorney and leading member of Georgia's Republican Party. "I'll be curious to see if these drugs will become harder to get."

Robert Blecker, a professor of criminal law, constitutional history, and the Eighth Amendment at New York Law School, told *NCR* that the question of midazolam was merely a make-way controversy that happens to be the "issue of the moment."

"Now that's passed, so we move back to the more vital question, which is the legitimacy of the death penalty," he said. "If you're going to say it's unconstitutional, then say it's unconstitutional. But to pretend that it's an open question, and then at the same time say, 'Well, any previous method would of course be inhumane'—it's absurd."

Despite being a public supporter of the death penalty, Blecker, who wrote *The Death of Punishment: Searching for Justice among the Worst of the Worst*, has long been against lethal injection, "not because it might cause pain, but because it certainly causes confusion; it conflates punishment with medicine. This is killing we're talking about. This is not medicine."

For that reason, he advocates for firing squads, saying they are "more overtly and honestly presenting what they really are, which is punishment … Let's acknowledge what we're doing, and if we can't stomach it, then abolish it."

Over the past 30 years, Blecker—a self-described retributivist—has visited more than two dozen prisons in 10 states and said the comfortable living arrangements for those sentenced to life without parole is largely why he supports the death penalty. For example, some prisons allow inmates to participate in softball leagues or have vacation days. "This is the living hell that awaits them if you abolish the death penalty."

"The problem is we declare 'let the punishment fit the crime,' then in the actual administration of criminal justice, we do everything we can to undermine it. The death penalty is the only self-avowed punishment we have left," he said, noting that not a single mission statement in any U.S. correctional facility includes the word "punishment."

Agreeing with Alito's opinion on *Glossip* v. Gross, Blecker added that the Constitution should not have to guarantee a painless death for the condemned, as nobody gets that assurance when experiencing natural death.

Recalling the lethal dosage his father-in-law received when dying of cancer, Blecker said the "exact same scene" was replicated when he witnessed the execution of Florida's Bennie Demps: strapped in a gurney, IV in his arm and surrounded by loved ones.

"How we kill those we detest should in no way resemble how we kill those we love," Blecker said. "We should acknowledge what we're doing."

But Michael Sheedy, executive director of the Florida Conference of Catholic Bishops, told *NCR* how someone is executed is irrelevant to the moral question.

"If it were painless, we'd still oppose the use of it in the current context," Sheedy said. "It continues to advance the misguided notion that killing is wrong by killing."

Archbishop Paul Coakley of Oklahoma City—where the Supreme Court case originated—released a statement following the decision:

> Even as we seek justice for these grave wrongs and render compassion for those who have endured great loss, our faith impels us to call for the building up of a culture of life where every human life is valued.

While the church maintains the immorality of executions, others oppose it for its impracticality. Burge, who recognizes that his party is known for being "tough on crime," said legislators in Georgia are taking a second look at capital punishment for its ineffectiveness. They've reduced sentences for nonviolent crimes and have made parole "more intelligent," and the state's conservatives are willing to apply the same scrutiny toward the death penalty.

"It's not a clean, simple system that people imagine it to be," he said. "It doesn't protect society the way people think. It's expensive, messy, it takes forever to implement, and I don't think it helps the victims. We're executing people 20 or 30 years after their crime—there's no deterrent in that … We're spending a whole lot of money on something that doesn't give us a very efficient value compared to the alternative: long-term imprisonment."

To which Blecker would answer, "Justice ain't cheap," emphasizing that if the "only proportional response to most cases is death as punishment, then even if it's very expensive, that's a price we should be willing to pay."

Kent Scheidegger, legal director of the Criminal Justice Legal Foundation, told *NCR* that the legal process in sentencing someone to death "does not have to be as long or as expensive as it is," as there is seldom any question as to the identity of the perpetrator in most capital cases. "There is no reason that sentences cannot be carried out within six years of sentence."

Mikulich, however, said about 4 percent of the people executed are innocent, also noting the 40 percent margin of error in federal cases. And about 10 percent of those sentenced to death since 1976 have been exonerated.

The same day the Supreme Court ruled on lethal injections, Glenn Ford—who spent 30 years on Louisiana's death row until his exoneration for a crime he did not commit—died after battling cancer for 15 months. Ford was released in March 2014 after a state district judge voided his conviction after evidence revealed that he did not commit a 1983 murder. The state compensated him for his years lost, but shortly after his release, Ford was diagnosed with cancer.

In a statement following Ford's death, the National Coalition to Abolish the Death Penalty wrote, "We pledge to continue the fight to abolish the death penalty in his honor."

"The death penalty is on the outs, with even conservative states like Nebraska outlawing the policy," the coalition wrote in a separate statement regarding Monday's ruling. "Yet that message clearly hasn't risen up to the highest court in the land. That means our work is far from done."

"Americans from all walks of life must recommit ourselves to ensuring that policymakers, attorneys, and yes, the Supreme Court understand America doesn't want or need the death penalty anymore."

NCR, which has advocated for abolishing the death penalty in editorials, filed a friend of the court brief in favor of the plaintiffs in the *Glossip v. Gross* case.

11

Lethal Injections Aren't More Humane

Joel B. Zivot

Dr. Zivot is a professor of anesthesiology and surgery at Emory University School of Medicine and the Fellowship Director in Critical Care Medicine. Among his areas of expertise are bioethics, advance directives, end of life care, and physicians and the death penalty.

The lethal injection is considered a more evolved way to mete out capital punishment than older, more violent, methods like the electric chair and public hanging. However, medical evidence and study of the drugs used both suggest that the press for lethal injections is just a comfortable lie, intended to make capital punishment more palatable to people who might otherwise object to its continued use as a legal punitive tool and deterrent to further crime.

Abstract

The death penalty by lethal injection is a legal punishment in the United States. Sodium thiopental, once used in the death penalty cocktail, is no longer available for use in the United States as a consequence of this association. Anesthesiologists possess knowledge of sodium thiopental and possible chemical alternatives. Further, lethal injection has the look and feel of a medical act thereby encouraging physician participation and comment. Concern has been raised that the death penalty by lethal injection, is cruel. Physicians are ethically directed to prevent cruelty within

"The absence of cruelty is not the presence of humanness: physicians and the death penalty in the United States," by Joel B. Zivot, *Philosophy, Ethics, and Humanities in Medicine,* 2012, 7:13. https://doi.org/10.1186/1747-5341-7-13 © Zivot; licensee BioMed Central Ltd. 2012. CC BY 2.0

the doctor-patient relationship and ethically prohibited from participation in any component of the death penalty. The US Supreme Court ruled that the death penalty is not cruel per se and is not in conflict with the 8th amendment of the US constitution. If the death penalty is not cruel, it requires no further refinement. If, on the other hand, the death penalty is in fact cruel, physicians have no mandate outside of the doctor patient relationship to reduce cruelty. Any intervention in the name of cruelty reduction, in the setting of lethal injection, does not lead to a more humane form of punishment. If physicians contend that the death penalty can be botched, they wrongly direct that it can be improved. The death penalty cocktail, as a method to reduce suffering during execution, is an unverifiable claim. At best, anesthetics produce an outward appearance of calmness only and do not address suffering as a consequence of the anticipation of death on the part of the condemned.

Body

Sodium thiopental, a drug once standard in the practice of anesthesiology, is no longer available in the USA. This is due to concerns by the manufacturer over use in the death penalty via lethal injection. [a]Anesthesiologists possess the pharmacological and technical expertise required to utilize alternatives to sodium thiopental injection in the setting of medical practice. From a technical and pharmacological perspective, the death penalty, by lethal injection, appears to possess common elements to the practice of Anesthesiology. As a consequence, death penalty proponents have sought advice from anesthesiologists and derive benefit both from the applicable knowledge possessed in the medical practitioner and the ability to usurp a civilized image by association. Death penalty opponents have used the 8th amendment of the US constitution as justification against the death penalty.[1,2] The argument asserts that death by injection would constitute cruel and unusual punishment. Indeed, evidence exists that the death penalty by lethal injection, as practiced in the

United States, falls below the standard of veterinary euthanasia[3] or the normal conduct of an anesthetic performed within a medical setting.[4] States that practice the death penalty have attempted to answer this concern by asserting that the death penalty is in fact constitutional by imposing a standard of humanness.[5] This paper will address the following concerns: First, what is meant by cruelty in the context of the death penalty? Second, what are the moral duties and obligations of the physician, both as doctor and citizen, with respect to conduct in society? Last, what is the role of the physician with respect to mitigation of cruelty and promotion of humanness in the setting of the death penalty?

It is important to draw the distinction between cruel acts and cruel individuals. When we say that a person is "cruel" we are referring to their motives. They want to inflict pain on others, take pleasure in the pain of others, or are indifferent to the pain of others. When we say that an action is cruel we are referring to its consequences: it causes unnecessary or excessive pain. Cruel people are prone to engage in cruel practices but sometimes kind and gentle people engage in cruel practices from a professed motive of mercy: they want to diminish the pain/suffering involved in the cruel practices. Cruel punishment was defined by the original framers of the constitution according to the prevailing notions of the time. The legal system recognizes that cruelty will always reflect a standard commensurate with the maturation of a civil society and that punishment should be proportionate to the severity of the crime. The U.S. Supreme Court has held that the death penalty itself is not inherently cruel, but has described it as "an extreme sanction, suitable to the most extreme of crimes."[6] It is important to recognize that constitutional protection is concerned with the method of punishment, not what is considered as the necessary suffering inherent in any method utilized to end a life humanely.[7] The court has considered the death penalty from a consequentialist perspective, that is, fundamentally, the death penalty is successful when the result is death of the condemned. From time to time, as society evolves, the court will evaluate the method of execution against the current cruelty standard only, not the rightness or wrongness of the death penalty.

In the setting of the doctor-patient relationship, medical ethics directs the physician to act without maleficence, that is, to do no harm. Is it reasonable that a physician, acting in ones own professional capacity, has no moral duty/obligation to anyone other than the patient? Many would argue that physicians have multiple other obligations, e.g., to public health and safety, to obey the law, the duty to warn, the duty to report, and various other public-spirited duties. On occasion, military physicians have duties that potentially place them in situations where medical ethics and military interests collide. Physicians' desire to reduce cruelty in the setting of the death penalty may be compared to the actions of military physicians' who use medical knowledge to enhance prisoner interrogation, resolve hunger strikes and prescribe psychotropic medications to retain soldiers in combat areas or accelerate a return to active duty.[8] Rather than affirming the universal ethical duties of physicians, recent Department of Defense memoranda create vagueness by distinguishing treating from non-treating physicians,[9] in order to justify participation of non-treating physicians in using their medical knowledge to inflict cruelty. The American Medical Association, Council on Ethical and Judicial Affairs, adopted the World Medical Association Declaration of Tokyo (1975)[10] which refutes the claim that physician participation in torture or other coercive, non-therapeutic activities benefits the detainee by affording some form of protection.[11] Physicians are citizens, but in a free society, the adherence to a rule is not inviolate. The conduct of a citizen allows thoughtful dissent from certain activities. A physician may refuse to perform certain military duties as a form of conscientious objection. With regard to the death penalty, physician refusal carries a higher moral authority than participatory complicity. Moral self-deception is created when a small purpose close at hand interferes with a greater purpose, perhaps more distant.[12]

David Waisel makes the case for physician involvement in the death penalty by lethal injection from the perspective of "humanness."[13] He refers to numerous reports of executions that proceeded with difficulties including problems with intravenous access,[10, 11] subjective assessments by observers that suffering occurred in the condemned,[14] and drug and dosage errors.[15] The claim that the death penalty by lethal injection can be botched suggests that it can therefore be improved. The appeal for improvement in the name of humaneness succeeds in drawing physicians in,[16] by appealing to a sympathetic concern for the welfare of others. From the above considerations of ethics and cruelty, the argument in support of humanness fails for several reasons. Physicians who participate in the death penalty are not concerned with prolonging life. This would certainly be the basic activity of medical practice. Physician participation then is in the name of mercy, or a reduction in the cruelty of lethal injection, except when it addresses that the purpose of the injection is to produce death. How cruel are the details of lethal injection apart from the lethality itself? By how much does a doctor's intervention reduce cruelty during execution? Non-physicians can establish intravenous access, and are able to draw up and inject medication. Non-physicians can provide comfort to the condemned as they anticipate and finally approach the execution table. It is conceivable that physician participation might increase cruelty from the perspective of the condemned. Physician endorsement of execution is so counter to normal medical practice that in the prisoners final moments, all vestiges of hope of a better society, should that be imagined, would be lost. Ultimately, the assertion that physician participation reduces cruelty is unverifiable. Only outwardly does it seem so by the witnesses. The administration of the death penalty is absolutely silent on the experience of the witness and needs not be addressed further.

Physicians are ethically directed to act with beneficence, and humanness may be subsumed within beneficence. Beneficence and humanness, as acts of conduct by physicians, are only directives within the doctor-patient relationship. Though acting humanely as a general activity may benefit society, it is not enforceable as a general standard of human conduct. If it is asserted that physicians are required to perform humane actions outside of the doctor-patient relationship, operationalizing such activity would be impossible. Within the complete rendering of human affairs, much inhumanity exists. No method exists to rank order humane tasks yet some method of humane triage would be required. If physicians position themselves as possessing statutory requirement for humane intervention in all affairs, they would otherwise be rightly accused of acting in one area at the seemingly arbitrary, or value laden, neglect of another. Physicians, like all citizens, may choose to act with humanity. Physicians may claim that in certain circumstances, they are not acting as a physician but as a private citizen.

Arguing that within the context of the death penalty the physician is a private citizen acting with "humanness" is flawed. Physician involvement is sanctioned by the state because physicians posses the medical knowledge of the components of lethal injection. Physicians, however, are not able to separate their medical knowledge and conduct in circumstances that possess the look and feel of a medical act. The death penalty does not claim to be a medical act and is therefore not subject to the standards within the performance of medical acts. Yet, it has chosen to usurp the tools of the medical trade thereby misleading physicians to believe they are working within the framework of medicine, and the public to believe that civility and safe oversight are in place.

Physicians are unambiguously prohibited from active participation in the death penalty according to the American Medical Associations opinion on capital punishment.[17] In the United States, only 20% of physicians are members of the AMA.[18] Additionally, only 7 of the 35 states that use the death penalty have statutory or regulatory incorporation of AMA ethical guidelines.[19] States have successfully barred medical boards from disciplining physicians who have been involved with the death penalty.[20] The AMA is limited in ability to punish physicians who are at odds with AMA policy beyond revocation of AMA membership. AMA membership is not a requirement by physicians to obtain medical licensure or practice medicine. State governments affirm legal authority in the regulation of medical practice, even in circumstance where the state medical board objects. In this regard, medical ethical conduct and state legal authority are at odds. The Nuremberg defense has clearly defined that medical practice, outside of ethical conduct is not made right by state fiat.[21]

The death penalty by lethal injection is a two-fold process. First, a state government acquires a chemical, or a combination of chemicals that when injected, causes death in people. Second, these chemicals are given as a punishment to individuals who have been lawfully convicted of certain offences with the purpose of causing them to die. In this situation, the convicted individual is not a patient and therefore physicians have no role in this activity. Physicians are neither capable nor required to remove cruelty in circumstances outside of the doctor-patient relationship. Physicians as citizens are not charged with the promotion of humanness outside of the practice of medicine. Physicians therefore have no obligation or mandate to be involved. It remains the states prerogative to execute individuals but it should be prohibited from using words or methods that are terms of art, which are used by physicians to describe medical practice.

In summary, physicians have no ethical requirement to participate in the death penalty. Fundamentally, any invocation of a reduction in suffering consequent to physician activity should exist within a doctor-patient relationship. A physician and a condemned prisoner have no doctor-patient relationship in the context of the administration of the death penalty by lethal injection. If, according to the United States Supreme Court, the death penalty is not cruel per se, it needs no improvement. If the death penalty is cruel, then attempts to reduce cruelty by pharmacological adjustments are not necessarily humane, or worse, create an illusion of humanness as they are physician directed.

Endnotes

ᵃ http://www.ashp.org/drugshortages/current/bulletin.aspx?id=563

References

1. Constitution of the United States: *Amendment 8—Cruel and Unusual Punishment*. 1791.

2. Baze ET, et al.: *REES, COMMISSIONER, KENTUCKY DEPARTMENT OF CORRECTIONS, ET AL. CERTIORARI TO THE SUPREME COURT OF KENTUCKY No. 07–5439.* 2008. Argued January 7, 2008—Decided April 16, 2008

3. Ty A: *Anesthetizing the Public Conscience: Lethal Injection and Animal Euthanasia, Fordham Urban Law Journal.* Fordham University Law School, 140 W. 62nd Street New York, NY 10023 USA; 2008:817-856.

4. Koniaris LG, Zimmers TA, Lubarsky DA, Sheldon JP: Inadequate anaesthesia in lethal injection for execution. *Lancet* 2005,365(9468):1412-1414. 10.1016/S0140-6736(05)66377-5 10.1016/S0140-6736(05)66377-5

5. IN RE KEMMLER, 136 U.S. 436. 1890. 136 U.S. 436 Google Scholar

6. Georgia GV 1976. 428 U.S. 153 96 S. Ct. 2909 (1976) U.S. LEXIS 82 49 L. Ed. 2d 859.

7. Resweber FV 1947. Louisiana ex rel., 329 U.S. 459, 67 S. Ct. 374, 916 L. Ed. 422.

8. Annas CL, Annas GJ, Contemp J: Enhancing the fighting force: medical research on American soldiers. *J Contemp Health L & Pol'y* 2009., 283: Spring

9. Keram EA: Will medical ethics be a casualty of the war on terror? *J Am Acad Psychiatry Law* 2006, 34: 6-8.

10. Chapman R: Witnesses describe killer's 'macabre' final few minutes. *Chicago Sun-Times* 1994., 5:

11. Darick Demorris W: *Brief for Darick Demorris Walker as Amicus Curiae Supporting Petitioner at 7, Hill v. McDonough, 547 U.S. 573.* 2006. WL558286

12. Martin MW: Self-Deception and Morality. *University Press of Kansas* 1986., 1:

13. David Waisel MD: Physician Participation in Capital Punishment. *Mayo Clin Proc* 2007,82(9):1073-1080. 10.4065/82.9.1073 10.4065/82.9.1073

14. Whoriskey P, Geis S: Lethal injection is on hold in 2 states. *The Washington Post* 2006, A1.

15. Provance J, Hall C: Problems bog down execution of Clark. *Toledo Blade* 2006, A1.

16. Zimmers TA, Lubarsky DA: Physician participation in lethal injection executions. *Curr Opin Anaesthesiol* 2007,20(2):147-151. 10.1097/ACO.0b013e3280895ab7 10.1097/ACO.0b013e3280895ab7

17. Opinion 2.06: Capital Punishment: *Current Opinions of the Council on Ethical and] udicial Affairs of the AMA.* American Medical Association, Chicago, IL; 1992.

18. Maves MD: *Chief Executive Officer, American Medical Association, A challenge to the House of Delegates.* Available at (Nov. 8, 2008) http://www.ama-assn.org/ama/pub/news/speeches/challenge-house-del-egates.shtml Available at (Nov. 8, 2008)

19. Ty A: The role of state medical boards in regulating physician participation in executions. *J Med Licensure Discip* 2009,95(3):7.

20. http://www.deathpenaltyinfo.org/north-carolina-supreme-court-overrules-state-medical-boards-ban-doctor-participation-executions

21. King HT Jr: The Legacy of Nuremberg. *Case West J Int Law* 34(Fall 2002):335e.

12

Changing the Code of Ethics Could End the Death Penalty

Tara Culp-Ressler

Tara Culp-Ressler is a senior editor at ThinkProgress with a focus on faith-based politics. She's worked with religious-themed non-profit organization like Faith in Public Life, the National Religious Campaign Against Torture, and Interfaith Voices.

Following the controversy of physician involvement in executions, there has been a push to change the code of ethics for the American Pharmacist Association in the hopes that it will lead to a cessation of lethal injection production and distribution. If this change happens, countries around the world will have to reconsider how to execute inmates—and decide which people can monitor the executions if doctors and pharmacists are no longer allowed. Other options range from a firing squad to gas chambers, though neither of these cruel options settles well with anyone.

Dennis McGuire struggled, choked, and gasped for air before he finally died, as his adult children watched on in horror. The state of Ohio used a never-before-used mix of drugs to kill him, and he appeared to slowly suffocate to death. Witnesses said the process took about 25 minutes, making it the longest execution since the state reinstituted capital punishment 15 years ago.

"One Sentence That Could Help End The Death Penalty In America," by Tara Culp-Ressler, ThinkProgress, April 10, 2014. Reprinted by Permission.

When Kelsey Kauffman, a retired Indiana resident and progressive activist, saw the headlines about McGuire—whose death sparked widespread outrage about the nature of lethal injections in the United States—she wanted to do something in response. So Kaufmann started a petition through SumOfUs, a group that allows citizens to organize to advance social justice causes.

Her ask? Get the American Pharmacist Association to add a sentence to its code of ethics to explicitly ban its members from participating in executions.

It may seem like a strange way to respond specifically to McGuire's case, but this one change could be an indirect method of inching the country toward putting an end to executions altogether. "The Association could help put a stop to the manufacturing and supplying of drugs used for lethal injections," Kauffman's petition, which garnered more than 36,000 signatures, explains, "and help end the use of the death penalty in the U.S. once and for all."

"I was reading an article last July about an execution that was postponed in Georgia because the Department of Corrections wouldn't give any information to the lawyers or the judges about what execution drugs were going to be used and where they had gotten them from. The article mentioned that pharmacists, unlike other medical professionals, are not banned from participating in executions. And I remember thinking—wow, that's surprising," Kauffman recounted in an interview with ThinkProgress. "I happen to be opposed to the death penalty. But I'm especially opposed to the medicalization of the death penalty."

Almost all major medical associations—the American Medical Association, the American Public Health Association, the American Board of Anesthesiology, and the American Nurses Association—prohibit their members from assisting in executions. These professional associations believe that taking another person's life against their will is a violation of the Hippocratic Oath, and can't be reconciled with health workers' ethical obligation to care for their patients. There can be stiff penalties for violating that. The American Board of Anesthesiology, which updated its policy in this area just four years ago, stipulates that members who participate in executions will lose their medical certification.

But, while the American Pharmacist Association (APhA) has a similar code of ethics, the issue of executions isn't specifically mentioned.

Kauffman believes that's an oversight, not a calculated policy position.

"It hasn't been an issue until now," she said. It used to be that "when executions took place, you just got your drugs from some European distributor. You didn't have doctors or nurses helping because they're banned, so a lot of the problems with executions have centered around the fact that you have incompetent people doing physical executions—they can't find veins, for example. But it's not been a question of pharmacists."

A controversy that hinges on pharmacies

Over the past few years, that's changed. In 2011, the European Commission imposed tight restrictions on the export of certain drugs used in executions, citing ethical issues with the death penalty. A growing number of the European and Asian companies that make those drugs are now refusing to sell them for use in executions, too. This international opposition to capital punishment has left American states scrambling to get the drugs they need to continue executing inmates. And it's meant that a small group of pharmacists are now participating in the executions.

States are turning to so-called "compounding pharmacies"—facilities that are outside of the regulatory scope of the Food and Drug Administration—to get the ingredients they need for untested cocktails like the one that killed McGuire. Compounding pharmacies, which repackage drugs to keep down the cost of filling prescriptions, are already controversial from a public health perspective. For instance, in 2012, a compounding pharmacy was identified as the source of a deadly meningitis outbreak that killed 36 people. Since then, Congress has worked to crack down on these unregulated facilities, although some public health advocates don't believe the recent legislative push goes far enough.

Some compounding pharmacies have agreed to manufacture the drugs that states need to kill people, but state officials won't always reveal the details. States like Oklahoma and Missouri claim that publicizing where they're getting their lethal drugs will result in too much public pressure on the compounding pharmacies to stop producing them. So the methods they're using for executions are increasingly kept secret, and it's not entirely clear whether they're violating the Constitution's prohibition against "cruel and unusual punishment."

Kauffman hopes that, if the American Pharmacist Association adopts a new policy position that forbids pharmacists from assisting in executions, this will all become moot because the employees at compounding facilities won't be able to continue supplying these drugs. And, after attending APhA's annual meeting at the end of last month, Kauffman believes senior officials in the pharmaceutical industry are receptive.

"I look at the American Pharmacist Association as a partner in this process, and when it comes to almost all of the pharmacists I spoke to, I see them as future allies," she said, pointing out that medical professionals don't have to be personally opposed to the death penalty to agree that it's against their code of ethics to participate in them.

Dr. Leonard Edloe is one of those allies. Edloe, who now serves as a pastor in Virginia after owning and operating a community pharmacy for four decades, received a lifetime achievement award from the APhA at its most recent meeting. He believes very firmly in the policy change regarding lethal injection.

"I've always been against this method of execution," Edloe said. "We're supposed to be about healing, and this is the exact opposite of that. I don't think most pharmacists are aware of the policy. They should be supportive of this campaign."

The push to change APhA's policy has also won the support of most of the country's major human rights organizations. Amnesty

International, the American Civil Liberties Union, Human Rights Watch, the NAACP, and the United Methodist Church are all co-sponsors of SumOfUs' campaign, and have signed onto a letter that was sent to the association at the end of last month regarding the issue.

"I hope the Association takes a position that says we're against it, and then pharmacists have enough ethical backbone to go along with it," Edloe added.

The medical community's problems with lethal injections

To the average American, lethal injection may seem like the best, most humane option for the people on death row. But that's not necessarily the case.

Since pharmacists are the sole hold-out in this area, the health workers who typically ensure that injections are administered properly are barred from overseeing executions. With no experts in the room, the process can go awry.

Medical professionals don't mince words about what that means in practice. At the end of last year, an anesthesiologist published an op-ed calling for the abolishment of lethal injection as a method of killing inmates, claiming that "what appears as humane is theater alone."

"States may choose to execute their citizens, but when they employ lethal injection, they are not practicing medicine. They are usurping the tools and arts of the medical trade and propagating a fiction," anesthesiologist Dr. Joel Zivot wrote in *USA Today* last December. He went on to explain that the drug shortages and the heightened secrecy surrounding compounding pharmacies have created an environment in which inmates are suffering painful deaths. Zivot believes that, if states want to continue executing people, they must return to the firing squad or the electric chair.

Writing in Slate, another medical professional, Dr. Matt McCarthy, agrees. "Part of the problem is the terminology: Words like *injection* and *cocktail* and *gurney* give the illusion that this form of capital punishment is civil," McCarthy points out. "This allows, regrettably, for a softening of the perception of what is actually happening: Medications that were designed to heal have been repurposed to kill."

Even the doctor who developed the original three-drug cocktail that has been used in lethal injections since 1977 has publicly come out against it. In 2007, three decades after Dr. Jay Chapman developed what he thought was the most humane method of ending a life, he suggested that the formula should be revisited—pointing out that it's a complicated method that can fail in the hands of prison officials who aren't medical experts.

"The simplest thing I know of is the guillotine. And I'm not at all opposed to bringing it back," he said at the time.

Chapman's suggestion brings up a central issue with capital punishment: The moral questions surrounding the death penalty come into sharp focus when inmates' lives are ended in more obviously violent and graphic ways. And that's exactly what the SumOfUs campaign is counting on.

Running out of options

Putting a definitive end to lethal injections means that states will have to find an alternate method for killing inmates. The majority of the states that still allow the death penalty don't sanction another method for executing inmates other than lethal injection. So that would require getting the legislature to pass a bill to approve one.

But the other options—gas chambers, guillotines, hanging, fire squads—aren't necessarily palatable to the American public. Even the states that technically have back-up methods on the books, like Missouri, which authorizes the use of a gas chamber to execute inmates, face significant roadblocks to actually putting that type of capital punishment method into practice.

"The [Missouri] attorney general last year asked the governor to request an appropriation of a million dollars to build a gas chamber. The governor, who's very pro-death penalty, basically said—are you kidding me? In 2014, we're going to build a gas chamber in Missouri? Forget about it," Kauffman recounted. "The gas chamber is simply not going to come back."

Similarly, Americans likely won't be excited about bringing back hanging, which evokes the United States' history of lynching black men. Virginia recently began pushing for the electric chair, but that bill stalled after an executioner testified against it, saying that electrocution isn't a good option because it often leaves inmates' bodies burned and blistered. And although some lethal injection opponents are joining Dr. Jay Chapman in arguing for the guillotine, which is the only method of execution that would allow inmates' organs to be harvested, it's not clear that Americans would actually have the stomach for that—particularly since public support for the death penalty as a whole has already plummeted to a 40-year low. States are running out of real options.

Kauffman believes the most realistic alternative is probably a firing squad. It's certainly still gruesome, but it wouldn't present ethical issues of medical professionals' participation or counsel, since we already train people to be sharpshooters. It's not just a hypothetical—at the beginning of this year, lawmakers in Missouri and Wyoming made headlines for proposing authorizing firing squads.

So execution by gunfire may be exactly where the states that don't seem likely to give up capital punishment, like Texas and Louisiana, are headed. But that could also make those states seem particularly extreme.

"Just getting lethal injections banned does not end the death penalty. We're well aware of that," Kauffman acknowledged. "You've got these outlier states that are really into the death penalty, and they're just going to switch to something else. But they're also going to make themselves even more isolated than they already are. I think at some point, they're going to be so few in number that the Supreme Court is going to say that the prevailing morality in the nation is that we no longer do these executions."

13

Innocent People Can Receive the Death Penalty

Nicole Colson

Nicole Colson is a reporter for Socialist Worker and a contributor to the International Socialist Review and CounterPunch. She frequently writes about civil liberties, the environment, women's rights and culture.

The case of Cameron Todd Willingham is one that challenges the effectiveness of the death penalty on multiple levels. Willingham was falsely accused of killing his three children and then found innocent after his execution, calling into question the expertise of forensic scientists on the case as well as the entire system that allowed Willingham to die at the hands of the state. Though Supreme Court Justice Antonin Scalia has since died, his 2005 assertion that an innocent person has never been executed in the United States continues to haunt those who know otherwise.

Cameron Todd Willingham was executed by the state of Texas for a crime that he didn't commit.

That is the conclusion of a lengthy investigation published this month in the *New Yorker*. In devastating detail, reporter David Grann lays out the facts of a case that contains all the familiar hallmarks of wrongful convictions—junk science, inept defense lawyers, a jailhouse snitch, and a court system designed to make it next-to-impossible for the innocent to clear their names.

Willingham was executed on February 17, 2004. He was convicted of setting a December 23, 1991, fire that killed his three young daughters—2 year-old Amber and 1-year-old twins, Karmon and Kameron—while his wife Stacy went to the Salvation Army to buy the children Christmas presents.

Witnesses at the scene described Willingham as frantic to save the children. Neighbors who saw the smoke ran to the house and found Willingham on the porch wearing only blue jeans, his chest blackened with soot, and his hair and eyelids singed from the fire. He had been trying to reach Amber, whose cries had awakened him. Once outside, he broke through the windows of the children's bedroom with a stick as neighbors called the fire department—but the flames were too intense.

He would later have to be restrained—eventually handcuffed—after repeatedly trying to run back into the house. "My babies are burning up!" neighbors heard him scream again and again. "My babies."

Willingham gave authorities permission to look through the house. "I know we might not ever know all the answers," he told authorities, "but I'd just like to know why my babies were taken from me."

But it wasn't long before Texas authorities were focusing on the idea that he had deliberately set the fire. His motive? According to Corsicana, Texas, District Attorney Pat Batchelor, "The children were interfering with his beer drinking and dart throwing."

Witnesses who had originally told how devastated Willingham had been by the fire changed their opinions as it became clear that investigators were focusing on him as a possible suspect—they now made much of his drinking and sometimes violent relationship with his young wife Stacy.

Fire investigators, who had concluded that the fire was started with a liquid accelerant, focused on the fact that Willingham had run out of the house barefoot—since if he had run outside by the path he claimed, he would have burned his feet. Since Willingham's feet were not burned, he must be guilty, investigators believed.

Two weeks after the fire, Willingham was arrested and charged with murder—because there were multiple victims, he qualified for the death penalty under Texas law.

In a story all-too-familiar in capital cases, Willingham, who was unemployed, had to rely on public defenders. A jailhouse snitch named Johnny Webb would also come forward to claim that Willingham admitted while in jail that he set the fire using lighter fluid.

John Jackson, then the assistant district attorney in Corsicana, was shocked when Willingham—whose own lawyers believed he was guilty—refused to take a plea deal that would have spared him the death penalty if he pled guilty.

According to Willingham's stepmother Eugenia, defense attorney David Martin (a former state trooper) showed her and her husband photographs of the burned children, saying, "Look what your son did. You got to talk him into pleading, or he's going to be executed."

But Cameron Todd Willingham refused. "I ain't gonna plead to something I didn't do, especially killing my own kids," he said.

During the subsequent two-day trial, as Grann wrote:

> The crux of the state's case...remained the scientific evidence gathered by [deputy fire marshal Manuel] Vasquez and [assistant fire chief Douglas] Fogg. On the stand, Vasquez detailed what he called more than "twenty indicators" of arson.
>
> "Do you have an opinion as to who started the fire?" one of the prosecutors asked.
>
> "Yes, sir," Vasquez said. "Mr. Willingham."
>
> The prosecutor asked Vasquez what he thought Willingham's intent was in lighting the fire. "To kill the little girls," he said.

Defense attorneys called just one witness to the stand—the Willingham's babysitter. It took a jury just one hour to find Cameron Todd Willingham guilty.

During the penalty phase of the trial, prosecutors went out of their way to portray Willingham as a "sociopath," focusing on the supposed meaning of Willingham's tattoo and the posters of rock bands hanging in the house. According to Grann:

> When [Willingham's wife] Stacy was on the stand, Jackson grilled her about the "significance" of Willingham's "very large tattoo of a skull, encircled by some kind of a serpent."
> "It's just a tattoo," Stacy responded.
> "He just likes skulls and snakes. Is that what you're saying?"
> "No. He just had—he got a tattoo on him."

The prosecution cited such evidence in asserting that Willingham fit the profile of a sociopath, and brought forth two medical experts to confirm the theory. Neither had met Willingham. One of them was Tim Gregory, a psychologist with a master's degree in marriage and family issues, who had previously gone goose hunting with Jackson, and had not published any research in the field of sociopathic behavior. His practice was devoted to family counseling.

At one point, Jackson showed Gregory Exhibit No. 60—a photograph of an Iron Maiden poster that had hung in Willingham's house—and asked the psychologist to interpret it. "This one is a picture of a skull, with a fist being punched through the skull," Gregory said; the image displayed "violence" and "death."

Gregory looked at photographs of other music posters owned by Willingham.

> "There's a hooded skull, with wings and a hatchet," Gregory continued. "And all of these are in fire, depicting—it reminds me of something like Hell. And there's a picture—a Led Zeppelin picture of a falling angel...I see there's an association many times with cultive-type of activities. A focus on death, dying. Many times, individuals that have a lot of this type of art have interest in satanic-type activities."

The other psychiatrist called by the state was James Grigson, who "testified so often for the prosecution in capital-punishment cases that he had become known as Dr. Death," according to Grann.

Three years after Willingham's trial, Grigson would be expelled from the American Psychiatric Association on ethics violations for repeatedly making a "psychiatric diagnosis without first having examined the individuals in question, and for indicating, while testifying in court as an expert witness, that he could predict with 100 percent certainty that the individuals would engage in future violent acts," Grann wrote.

Willingham, continued to fight to prove his innocence from behind bars—relying on the help of a prison pen-pal and friend Elizabeth Gilbert, who began corresponding with him in 1999 at the urging of a friend who was involved in anti-death penalty work. Gilbert began going over the facts of the case herself.

Interviewing jailhouse informant Johnny Webb, Gilbert found him to be paranoid. During Willingham's trial, he had admitted to being "mentally impaired" and having been diagnosed with post-traumatic stress disorder. According to Grann, just months after Gilbert visited Webb in 2000, Webb sent John Jackson, the assistant district attorney at the time of Willingham's trial, a Motion to Recant Testimony, declaring, "Mr. Willingham is innocent of all charges."

Willingham's lawyer was not informed of Webb's recantation, and soon after, Webb withdrew his recantation.

In 2004, Gilbert, along with Cameron Todd Willingham's relatives, persuaded a fire investigation expert, Gerald Hurst, to look at the evidence in the case. Point by point, Hurst systematically debunked the claims made by arson investigators Vasquez and Fogg. Instead of arson, Hurst found that the fire was most likely started by a space heater or faulty wiring. Of the supposed "20 indicators" of arson that investigators had found, Hurst believed only one was scientifically valid—and that there was an easy explanation for it.

But the report prepared by Hurst—who had already helped to exonerate 10 other wrongly convicted people—was ignored by officials. According to Grann:

> The Innocence Project obtained, through the Freedom of Information Act, all the records from the governor's office and

the board pertaining to Hurst's report. "The documents show that they received the report, but neither office has any record of anyone acknowledging it, taking note of its significance, responding to it, or calling any attention to it within the government," Barry Scheck said. "The only reasonable conclusion is that the governor's office and the Board of Pardons and Paroles ignored scientific evidence."

Days later, on February 13, the Texas Board of Pardons and Paroles denied Willingham's request for clemency.

LaFayette Collins, who was a member of the board at the time, explained the mindset of the board to Grann:

> "You don't vote guilt or innocence. You don't retry the trial. You just make sure everything is in order, and there are no glaring errors." He noted that although the rules allowed for a hearing to consider important new evidence, "in my time, there had never been one called." When I asked him why Hurst's report didn't constitute evidence of "glaring errors," he said, "We get all kinds of reports, but we don't have the mechanisms to vet them."

Willingham was put to death four days later on February 17, 2004.

"After his death," Grann wrote, "his parents were allowed to touch his face for the first time in more than a decade. Later, at Willingham's request, they cremated his body and secretly spread some of his ashes over his children's graves. He had told his parents, 'Please don't ever stop fighting to vindicate me.'"

Willingham's case has all the hallmarks of wrongful convictions—and since his death, the case for his innocence has only gotten stronger. Several fire experts who have re-examined the case in the years since Willingham's execution agreed with Hurst's opinion that the fire wasn't arson.

In 2005, Texas established a government commission to investigate allegations of error and misconduct by forensic scientists. Fire scientist Craig Beylor, who was hired by the commission, released a damning report into the Willingham case and that of another prisoner. In the report, wrote Grann, Beylor noted that investigators:

> "had no scientific basis for claiming that the fire was arson, ignored evidence that contradicted their theory, had no comprehension of flashover and fire dynamics, relied on discredited folklore, and failed to eliminate potential accidental or alternative causes of the fire. He said that Vasquez's approach seemed to deny "rational reasoning" and was more "characteristic of mystics or psychics.""

But scratch the surface of death penalty convictions in the U.S., and you'll find dozens of cases with equally stunning errors—particularly in Texas, the death penalty capital of the U.S.

According to a 2000 *Dallas Morning News* investigation, around one in every four inmates condemned to death in Texas was represented by court-appointed attorneys who had been "reprimanded, placed on probation, suspended or banned from practicing law by the State Bar" at some point in their careers.

The year after Cameron Todd Willingham was executed, the state of Texas sent Frances Newton to her death. Newton's attorney at her trial was Ron Mock, who was notorious for his shoddy work on death penalty cases. What's more, the crime lab destroyed evidence that could have been re-tested to prove Frances' innocence—including the clothes Frances was wearing the night of the murders she supposedly committed.

As the *Austin Chronicle* reported before her execution, "There is no incontrovertible evidence against Newton, and the paltry evidence that does exist has been completely compromised. Moreover, her story is one more in a long line of Texas death row cases in which the prosecutions were sloppy or dishonest, the defenses incompetent or negligent, and the constitutional guarantee of a fair trial was honored only in name."

In a 2005 Supreme Court decision, Justice Antonin Scalia scoffed at the idea that there had been—or would ever be—an innocent person executed in the U.S. "[I]n every case of an executed defendant of which I am aware, [DNA] technology has confirmed guilt," Scalia said, adding that there was not "a single case—not one—in which it is clear that a person was executed for a crime he did not commit."

The case of Cameron Todd Willingham is rare—not because he was an innocent man wrongly accused, but because he is being proven innocent after his execution, which has happened only very rarely because investigations into cases end after executions. (The Texas commission is likely to avoid the question of Willingham's actual innocence, focusing on investigators' procedural conduct instead.)

But even Willingham's innocence may not be enough to raise doubts about the death penalty for the likes of Scalia. This August, dissenting from a Supreme Court ruling granting Georgia death row inmate Troy Davis a new trial based on his claims of innocence (and the fact that seven of nine "witnesses" against Davis have since recanted), Scalia argued against stopping Davis' execution on the grounds that "this Court has never held that the Constitution forbids the execution of a convicted defendant who has had a full and fair trial, but is later able to convince a habeas court that he is 'actually' innocent."

In other words, the Supreme Court has never dared to question a lower court's decision and stopped the execution of an innocent person. Innocence doesn't matter.

Proponents of capital punishment like Scalia claim the system ultimately "works," but the family and friends of Cameron Todd Willingham—who was let down by the justice system at every turn—know that is a lie. With every new revelation about incompetent "experts," bungled investigations and wrongful convictions, that system is further exposed.

It's time to end the death penalty.

14

The Death Penalty Has Consequences for Families, Too

Federica Valabrega

Federica Valabrega is a freelance news photographer, originally based in Washington, D.C. and now sharing her time between New York City and Rome, Italy. Her breaking-news freelance work has appeared in the New York Times Magazine and on the Magnum Photos' web site.

Capital punishment impacts more than condemned prisoners. Often forgotten in death penalty cases are the families of sentenced inmates. They have to deal with grief while simultaneously being criminalized themselves and fighting against stereotypes. They are the collateral damage of the death penalty, and often live to suffer the consequences of their loved ones' crimes long after the prisoner has been put to death. Is there a way to punish a criminal without punishing their family, or is capital punishment by nature something that takes its pound of flesh from both the living and the dead?

Celia McWee, 83, looked forward to Saturdays for 13 years. This was her favorite day of the week because she would use it to make herself pretty for her Sunday morning visit. But she wouldn't go to church. She would visit the state prison. She would drive three hours from Augusta, Georgia, to Ridgeville, South Carolina, to visit her son, Jerry McWee. Jerry had been on death row since he robbed and killed John Perry, a grocery store clerk in rural Aiken County, in 1991. He was executed on April 14, 2004. He was 52.

"Saturday was an exciting day because it was my day to choose the outfit I was going to wear, to go to the beauty shop because I wanted to look my best for him," she said, crying. "And Sunday going up there was exciting because it was something to look forward to. But on the way back, it was nothing but tears."

For as long as her son was in prison, her weekly schedule kept her going, she said. On Mondays, Wednesdays, and Fridays, she would not leave the house until she received her son's phone call. Tuesdays and Thursdays were her days to go grocery shopping, do the laundry, and vacuum. And then came Sundays, when she would share a ride with other inmates' mothers to the prison. She would meet them at a gas station in Columbia, South Carolina.

Although her son was executed four years ago, not a day goes by that McWee does not recall the sound of his shackles dragging on the floor of the prison each time she visited him.

"The noise that most stands out in my mind is when they would bring them from one building to the other, and we could hear them walking with those chains around their ankles and around their waist and their wrists," she said. "That is torture. I mean, to see your son being brought in worse than you do to a dog."

McWee's house is filled with pictures of her son. She proudly reminisces about the day Jerry got married and when, despite having only a high school education, he joined the police force. Then she shows a black-and-white print of Jerry in an emergency medicine technician (EMT) uniform. After two years as a police officer and five as a firefighter, Jerry had decided to make his life all about helping others in need. That is when he went back to school to study emergency medicine.

"He was the kind of guy that would go out of his way to help others," she said. "He was a people person like me, used to helping the ones in need. Never would I have imagined this could have happened to my family. Everything was so nice and dandy, and it took so little time to turn things around. It is true he is in a much better place now, but I still feel he should be with me instead."

McWee's feeling is common to many relatives of inmates executed by the state. They are trying to recover from the trauma of waiting many years for their loved one's scheduled death. But often their suffering is made worse because many people still do not recognize their pain as legitimate.

Zipped wounds

Like McWee, Bill Babbitt had a tough recovery. His younger brother Manny, a decorated Vietnam War veteran severely affected by post-traumatic stress syndrome, was executed at San Quentin State Prison on his 50th birthday—May 3, 1999. He had been charged with robbing Leah Schendel, an elderly woman who died of a heart attack during the crime in Sacramento, California.

What makes Babbitt feel better is touring the country to talk about his brother's "unfair" execution; Babbitt is a member of Murder Victims' Families for Human Rights (MVFHR), a group founded in Philadelphia in 2004. The group offers support and advocacy for victims.

He gives his testimony using what he calls "the power of remembrance," letting his "zipped wound" open, and pouring out what he thinks needs to be said about Manny's case. He is trying to educate the public about why the death penalty was unnecessary in his brother's case. Yet many still consider his efforts to be those of a "second-class victim" who is defending a criminal, he said.

"My job is to educate and tell them, 'Hey, you lose a rabbit or a dog or a cat, and you grieve over it,'" he said. "'Manny was a human being. Why should I not grieve over him just as well?' It is the unfairness of that I have to talk about."

A Trail of Victims

The families who survive the state execution of their inmate relative are still not specifically referred to as "victims of abuse of power," as defined by the United Nations General Assembly's 1985 *Declaration of Basic Principles of Justice for Victims of Crime and Abuse of Power.*

Article 18 of the declaration defines a victim of abuse of power as a person "who, individually or collectively, [has] suffered harm, including physical or mental injury, emotional suffering, economic loss or substantial impairment of [his or her] fundamental rights, through acts or omissions that do not yet constitute violations of national criminal laws but of internationally recognized norms relating to human rights."

In some countries, including the United States, killing by lethal injection is not considered an abuse of power. The declaration does not include the death penalty as a "violation of internationally recognized norms relating to human rights."

"But these people [families of death row inmates] have, in many ways, suffered a trauma, and their experience, in many ways, parallels the experience of survivors of homicide victims," said Susannah Sheffer, director of No Silence, No Shame, a project of MVFHR.

The problem is that people don't think of the inmate as someone who might have a family who will grieve when he is executed.

"Families of the executed are invisible victims, hidden victims. People are not even thinking through the fact that when an execution is carried out, it's going to leave a grieving family," Sheffer said. "A lot of people hold the family responsible, kind of 'guilt by association.' They think this [the inmate] is a monster, so the parents must have created that."

Jerry McWee's mother said she is haunted by the image of her son strapped on the execution bed, blowing her the last kiss. She also said she was not the only one to suffer from her son's death.

"It is a horrible, horrible experience to have to go through for years. It not only punishes the inmates, it punishes so many people," said McWee. "One of Jerry's daughters, Misty, exactly one year after his execution, tried to commit suicide. She cut her wrists, because she said she had to be with her father and that she did not belong on this earth."

[...]

Studying Loss

Sandra Jones, a research sociologist and professor at Rowan University in New Jersey, released a study on the issues of grief and loss faced by the families with a relative on death row.

Jones spent years building relationships with families of death row inmates. She has taken it upon herself to bring kids of inmates to see their fathers in the Delaware County Prison in Pennsylvania when their own family members refuse to do so.

She became particularly close to Brian Steckel's family. Steckel was convicted of raping and killing 29-year-old Sandra Lee Long. Jones witnessed Steckel's execution in 2005. She is now writing a book about her personal experience with death row inmates' families. She said the government ignores these families because it feels guilty.

"If the system gave these families the attention they deserve, it would come across [as] really hypocritical, because they are the very system that is killing their loved ones," she said.

She also explains that the reason death row inmates' families are often forgotten is that the survivor victims themselves do not want to be put in the spotlight, since they feel guilty for and are ashamed of their loved ones' mistakes.

"The family gets criminalized along with their loved ones, and stigmatized to the extent that they don't feel comfortable coming out and demanding attention because they feel guilty. They have a lot of guilt and a lot of shame. They [ask] themselves what they could have done differently," she said.

"Writer Elizabeth Sharpen sometimes refers to them as the 'double losers,'" Jones said. "A lot of these guys on death row have murdered a wife or an uncle or somebody within the family, and so the surviving family members are put into this position where if they support and grieve the loss of the loved one on death row, they are made to feel they did not really love the one who was murdered."

Losing a child to the death penalty becomes a never-ending loss, one "similar to having a disabled child that you are grieving for every unmet milestone he misses throughout life," said Jones. It becomes a "wound that never heals and keeps opening up with every failed appeal."

Between losing a child to a murderer and losing one to death row—as is the case for McWee—the latter seems to be the more painful of the two because of the "never-ending wait."

Having to wait for your son to be executed is "horrible, because you know it is coming, but you don't know when," said McWee, whose son, Jerry, was executed 14 years after her daughter, Joyce, was murdered by Joyce's husband on December 31, 1980.

"[My daughter's murder] was a shock, but [it was] nothing compared to the death penalty hanging over your head for 13 years," she said. "News of her murder came unexpectedly, [but] the wait is horrible. One day he called me at 12:30, and he said, 'Mother, I have been served.' I had no idea what he meant. All I knew was that lunch was served at 11:30. So I said, 'What [do] you mean, you have been served? What did you eat for lunch?' So he said, 'Mother, you don't understand. I have been served with my death warrant—they have given me my day of execution.'"

Murder is Murder

Even murder victim families sympathize with state execution survivor families, finding it unjust that their pain is labeled differently from theirs.

The Rev. Walter Everett, a pastor at St. Jones United Methodist Church in Sunbury, Connecticut, lost his son, Scott, in 1987. Scott was murdered by Mike Carducci in Easton, Connecticut. The pastor has been part of MVFHR since it was founded. He said he feels close to parents whose children are on death row.

Everett said it is important to educate people about the death penalty without making a distinction about different victims. He travels around the country to speak about the experience he shares with many families whose loved ones have been executed under the death penalty.

"I see them just as much a 'victim' as I am. That person, regardless of what their son or daughter has done, or their loved ones, they still love them, so they become a victim when that person is killed," he said. "Since I got to know several people whose family members were executed, I see the pain they have gone through, and I believe their story should be told as much, because their pain is just as deep as my pain."

Everett took part in a vigil in California to stop the execution of Clarence Ray Allen, a 76-year-old, and at that point blind and in a wheelchair. Allen was put to death on January 17, 2006, for planning three murders from his cell while serving a life sentence.

"I went out there and I met his children. Lovely people. And they hurt, they pained as he went through that," he said.

Former death row inmates who have been exonerated share the belief that their families' grief rarely receives attention. Since executions now take place behind closed doors, the system has become "sterile," said Kirk Bloodsworth, the first person on death row to be exonerated because of DNA evidence.

Bloodsworth served nearly nine years in a Maryland prison for the 1984 rape and murder of nine-year-old girl he had never met.

"They don't want to show the 'crying mother' over the executed son. No matter what he has done, he is still paying for that, and they don't show that part of it," he said. "She has got no say. She raised a murderer. That is how they are looking at her, and that was not her fault, necessarily."

Bloodsworth regained his freedom on June 28, 1993, but his mother, Jeanette, did not live to see him walk out of prison. She died earlier that year. Bloodsworth was taken in chains to see her body, but prison officials refused to allow him to attend the funeral.

"My mother went through hell watching me. I was her son, and I was going to be executed, and nobody cared about a word she said. I thought that was a terrible way to have to treat somebody," he said.

Rob Warden is the director of the Center on Wrongful Conviction in Chicago, and has been a legal affairs writer for more than 25 years. He said that while the stories of inmates' family members are not necessarily ignored, the focus is often on the person "walking out of the door."

"The stories of relatives of wrongful conviction in general tend to be overlooked," he said, "because they are so overshadowed by the poignancy of the innocent person or the person who was executed himself."

This does not imply that these stories should not be told. On the contrary, they should not be forgotten, Warden said.

"We should understand that when we execute somebody, no matter how heinous that person might be, it is over for that person," said Warden. "But the pain that is inflicted on parents, or siblings, or children, is permanent. It is everlasting. It will be there. It is ongoing."

15

Problems with Today's Death Penalty System

Marc Hyden

Marc Hyden is a conservative political activist and an amateur Roman historian. He has served as the Legislative Liaison/Public Affairs Specialist for the State of Georgia and as the Legislative Aide to the Georgia Senate President Pro Tempore.

States are trying to figure out how to deal with problems the death penalty poses, but have yet to come up with any workable solutions. Innocent people who are wrongly executed also challenge moral and philosophical support of the practice. At least eighteen states to date have abolished capital punishment, acknowledging that the system is broken and archaic and largely unfixable no matter what policy changes are enacted. But what does that mean for the future of crime and punishment?

On the evening of March 11, 2014, Glenn Ford was released from Louisiana's death row after 30 years of captivity for a murder that he did not commit. The prosecution had withheld testimony that would have exonerated Ford and relied on faulty forensic analyses. Unfortunately, Ford's story is not unique. It is one of many cases that exemplify the problems with today's death penalty system.

Many states are grappling with the systemic dysfunction plaguing the current capital punishment regime, but they are finding it is difficult, if not impossible, to maintain such a program while reconciling its moral, pragmatic, and philosophical failures. The state ought not kill innocent citizens, but the death penalty carries an inherent and undeniable risk of doing precisely that. Whether through mistakes or abuse of power, innocent people routinely get sent to death row.

Some, like Ford, eventually get out: To date, 10 individuals in Louisiana and 144 nationally have been released from death row because they were wrongly convicted. Many others have been executed despite substantial doubts about the verdict.

The fiscal cost of the death penalty pales in comparison to the human cost, but local, state, and federal governments must justify all spending as they struggle with ongoing budgetary shortfalls. John DeRosier, Louisiana District Attorney for Calcasieu Parish, estimated that a capital case in Louisiana is at least three times more costly than a non-death case. Studies in North Carolina, Maryland, California, and many others show that capital punishment is many times more expensive than life without parole, and there's a long history of the death penalty pushing municipal budgets to the brink of bankruptcy and even leading to tax increases.

The fiscal impact of the death penalty is not lost on state governments. But they seem, broadly, more concerned with the fiscal impact than with the death part. Louisiana is currently considering House Bill 71, which is similar to Florida's "Timely Justice Act," which limits the appeals process. Had this legislation passed earlier, it would have likely led to numerous wrongful executions because it shortens the number of appeals available to death row inmates. Cutting the appeals process may, in the end, lead to modest cost savings, but the most expensive step in the death penalty process—pretrial activities and the actual trials—are unaffected by this legislation. And these are precisely the stages that produce wrongful convictions. Evidence proving them wrongful often emerges more than a decade after the initial trial, so the nominal savings are not worth the moral cost of executing an innocent person.

The expense passed on to the taxpayers and risk of killing innocent people are often both justified by claims that the death penalty saves lives—it supposedly deters murder and provides the justice that murder victims' families deserve. Multiple scientific studies have actually shown that the death penalty doesn't deter murder. Many murder victims' family members are vocally rejecting this program because it retraumatizes them through a decades-long process of trials, appeals, and constant media attention.

There's no greater authority than the power to take life, and our government currently reserves the authority to kill the citizens it's supposed to serve. This is the same fallible government responsible for the Tuskegee Experiment, overreach including NSA spying, and failures such as the Bay of Pigs. Of course, the death toll from wars government either started or intensified is staggering. Submitting the power to kill U.S. citizens to the State is unwise considering this history of error and malfeasance.

And states aren't even complying with the standards that allegedly keep the death penalty from falling afoul of the "cruel and unusual" punishment standard.

Many states can no longer obtain the previously used and approved death penalty drugs. So they've started experimenting on inmates with new drug combinations acquired from secret sources. This has led to botched, torturous executions. In Ohio, Dennis McGwire audibly struggled for 25 minutes before he died, and Clayton Lockett's execution in Oklahoma was postponed after he failed to die after 10 minutes. Indeed, Lockett only met his demise due to a heart attack, 30 minutes after the botched execution. Cruel and unusual?

Glenn Ford could have easily been subjected to the same experiences. Louisiana, like many other states, keeps the source of its death penalty drugs a secret. This secrecy calls into question the legality and validity of the drugs' manufacturers. We are far from the level of government transparency required to limit government abuse, misuse, and power.

Most people will agree that the death penalty system is not perfect—but a program designed to kill guilty U.S. citizens *must* be perfect because the Constitution demands zero errors. To date, 18 states and the District of Columbia have abandoned capital punishment, aware that the system is broken and finally convinced, after years of legislative, judicial, and policy "fixes," that it cannot be mended. Other states still believe they can make capital punishment work properly, but they continue to break an already failed program one "fix" at a time.

16

The Fate of the Death Penalty Abroad

Viasna

Viasna is a non-governmental human rights organization created in 1996 during mass protest actions of the democratic opposition in Belarus. Their primary goal is to contribute to development of the civic society in Belarus, based on respect to human rights and as described in the Universal Declaration of Human Rights and the Constitution of the Republic of Belarus.

In December of 2016, several world leaders and organizations met to discuss the future of capital punishment on a global level. Member nations of the Council of Europe have not engaged in capital punishment since 1997, but countries outside the council are slow to join the movement. Belarus, in particular, is struggling with the question of the death penalty and facing push-back from human rights organizations. For many countries, change will be gradual, experts say—and a direct and instant moratorium on the death penalty is unlikely.

A conference on the abolition of the death penalty and public opinion opened today in Minsk's Crowne Plaza Hotel. The event was organized by the Council of Europe in cooperation with the Ministry of Foreign Affairs of Belarus.

The conference brings together representatives of the Belarusian government, the Council of Europe Parliamentary Assembly

(PACE), the United Nations and other international organizations, the Belarusian Orthodox Church, international and Belarusian NGOs and the media.

Andrei Paluda and Valiantsin Stefanovich of the Human Rights Center "Viasna" were invited to the event despite strong opposition from the authorities, which prevented the human rights defenders from attending a similar forum in March 2016.

Andrei Paluda, coordinator of the campaign *Human Rights Defenders against the Death Penalty in Belarus*, said debates on the issue involved many references to historical and philosophical aspects, while he stressed it was the actual situation in the country that mattered most.

> "You know, many people said that Belarus had a de facto moratorium on the death penalty between the executions of Aliaksandr Hrunou and Siarhei Ivanou. But it is essential that Siarhei Ivanou was shot just a a few weeks after the conference, which was organized in March. And this conference takes place against the backdrop of the enforcement of four death sentences this year, three of which took place a month ago," Paluda said.

The human rights activist stressed the fact that many government representatives advocated cooperation with the Council of Europe, but the practice shows the opposite:

> "To date, there is no cooperation with international treaty bodies, which is confirmed by six decisions of the UN Human Rights Committee. None of them was taken into account, as well as the Committee's request for interim measures in respect of Henadz Yakavitski and Siarhey Khmialeuski. As a result, both have been executed."

Chairman of the first session, head of the Department of European Cooperation at the Ministry of Foreign Affairs Andrei Bushyla said in response that they were not yet approaching "a direct moratorium, but the humanization of legislation is gradually happening."

He said that according to a survey conducted by the Independent Institute of Socio-Economic and Political Studies in April of this year, 51% of respondents were in favor and 49% were against the death penalty.

Alexandre Guessel, Director of Political Affairs at the Council of Europe, stressed that talking of a de facto moratorium looked like saying that there could be a hunger strike between breakfast and lunch.

Valiantsin Stefanovich also noted that the human rights defenders sent copies of a recent report on the death penalty to all members of the House of Representatives. He said it was important to continue holding parliamentary hearings involving a wide range of public and human rights organizations.

> "I wish that was a particular message from the government in this regard, so that it could be clear if we have on the agenda a moratorium as such, or we'll keep talking a lot and continue applying the death penalty. The Belarusian authorities have not demonstrated that the question of the death penalty will be solved," Stefanovich said.

The Council of Europe has made the abolition of death penalty one of its priorities, and has been fighting it for decades. As a result, no execution has taken place in the Council of Europe's member States since 1997.

Belarus, which is not a member of the Council of Europe, is the only country in Europe that still applies death penalty. The first ever Council of Europe's Action plan for Belarus 2016-2017 stresses that "the abolition of the death penalty in Belarus remains the top priority for the CoE, as capital punishment is a major obstacle for Belarus to taking steps towards becoming a CoE member state."

Organizations to Contact

The editors have compiled the following list of organizations concerned with the issues debated in this book. The descriptions are derived from materials provided by the organizations. All have publications or information available for interested readers. The list was compiled on the date of publication of the present volume; the information provided here may change. Be aware that many organizations take several weeks or longer to respond to inquiries, so allow as much time as possible.

Amicus
PO Box 46101
London EC4V 6YT
DX 233 Chancery Lane
phone: 0207 072 5603 / 31
email: admin@amicus-alj.org
website: www.amicus-alj.org

Though based in London, Amicus seeks to provide representation for those who are facing the death penalty in the United States. Founded in 1992, they intend to raise awareness about justice and how the death penalty exploits those most vulnerable in society.

CEDP—Campaign to End the Death Penalty
PO Box 25730
Chicago Illinois, 60625
email: randi@nodeathpenalty.org
website: www.nodeathpenalty.org

The Campaign to End the Death Penalty (CEDP) pushes families and those affected by the death penalty to the front of their movement. They believe the only way to abolish the death penalty is through sharing the experiences of those who have suffered.

CJLF—Criminal Justice Legal Foundation
Criminal Justice Legal Foundation
2131 L Street, Sacramento, CA 95816
phone: 916.446.0345
fax: 916.446.1194
email: mr_temp@cjlf.org
website: www.cjlf.org

The Criminal Justice Legal Foundation (CJLF) exists to maintain a balance between the rights of crime victims and those who are accused. They want to ensure that appropriate action is taken for those who are convicted and all actions are carried out in an orderly and constitutional manner.

CMN—Catholic Mobilizing Network
Catholic Mobilizing Network
415 Michigan Avenue NE, Suite 210
Washington, DC 20017
phone: (202) 541-5290
email: info@catholicsmobilizing.org
website: catholicsmobilizing.org

The Catholic Mobilizing Network (CMN) believes that the death penalty should be abolished and pushes for more reformative methods to be used on criminals. They believe that education, advocacy, and prayer can make all the difference.

Death Penalty Focus
Death Penalty Focus
5 Third Street, Suite 725
San Francisco, CA 94103
phone: 415-243-0143 Fax: 415-766-4593
email: information@deathpenalty.org
website: deathpenalty.org

Death Penalty Focus pushes to abolish the death penalty through education, advocacy, and media outreach. Their reasons for their position are rooted in discrimination of prisoners, the cruel and infective treatment of the death penalty, and the need to provide preventative measures to crime. They publish a newsletter called The Focus that includes updated information about the death penalty as it happens.

ICDP—International Commission Against Death Penalty

Asunta Vivó Cavaller—*Executive Director*
Serrano Galvache, 26,
Torre Sur, 10 planta, Despacho 10-78,
28071 Madrid, Spain
phone: +00 34 91 3799458 Mobile: +00 34 646 902 738
email: info@icomdp.org
website: www.icomdp.org

The International Commission Against Death Penalty (ICDP) was founded in Madrid in 2010 after the Spanish Government launched an initiative to abolish the death penalty. The goal of the ICDP is to rid the death penalty from around the world. Their members have a wide range of backgrounds, both in decision-making and geographic representation.

NCADP—National Coalition to Abolish the Death Penalty

1620 L Street, NW, Suite 250
Washington DC, 20036
202-331-4090
email: admin-info@ncadp.org
website: www.ncadp.org

The National Coalition to Abolish the Death Penalty (NCADP) is dedicated to removing the death penalty as a form of punishment. Families of victims, former law enforcement officers and organizations promoting civil justice all pool their experiences together in order to provide a united political and legal front to end the death penalty.

SADP—Students Against Death Penalty

email: hooman@studentabolition.org
website: studentabolition.org

The Students Against Death Penalty (SADP) wants to end death penalty by promoting public education and youth activism. It is entirely made up of volunteers who engage in human rights and criminal justice reform.

TCADP—The Texas Coalition to Abolish the Death Penalty

2709 S Lamar
Austin, TX 78704
phone: 512 441-1808
email: khoule@tcadp.org
website: tcadp.org

The Texas Coalition to Abolish the Death Penalty (TCADP) was established in 1998, but grew to a full-fledged organization in 2008 after hiring a full time Executive Director and receiving proper funding. This group pushes to end the death penalty in Texas. They work together with local, state and national partners to reduce the death penalty sentence and share their concerns with elected officials.

WTI—Witness to Innocence

Witness to Innocence
1501 Cherry Street
Philadelphia, PA 19102
phone: 267-519-4584
email: info@witnesstoinnocence.org
website: www.witnesstoinnocence.org

Witness to Innocence (WTI) is the only organization that uses the voices of exonerated death row survivors to help abolish the death penalty. Their main goal is to use their members' voices to put an end to the death penalty through education about wrongful convictions.

Bibliography

Books

James R. Acker, *Questioning Capital Punishment: Law, Policy, and Practice*. New York, NY: Routledge, 2014.

Stuart Banner, *The Death Penalty: An American History*. Cambridge, MA: Harvard University Press, 2003.

Frank R. Baumgartner, Suzanna De Boef, and Amber E. Boydstun, *The Decline of the Death Penalty and the Discovery of Innocence*. Cambridge, MA: Cambridge University Press, 2008.

Elizabeth Beck, Sarah Britto, and Arlene Andrews, *In the Shadow of Death: Restorative Justice and Death Row Families*. Oxford, London: Oxford University Press, 2009.

Hugo Adam Bedau and Paul G. Cassell, *Debating the Death Penalty: Should America Have Capital Punishment?: The Experts on Both Sides Make Their Case*. Oxford, London: Oxford University Press, 2005.

Robert M. Bohm, *The Death Penalty Today*. Boca Raton, FL: CRC, 2008.

Scott Christianson, *Innocent Inside Wrongful Conviction Cases*. New York, NY: University Press, 2006.

David Garland, Randall McGowen, and Michael Meranze, *America's Death Penalty: Between past and Present*. New York, NY: University Press, 2016.

Craig Haney, *Death by Design Capital Punishment as Social Psychological System*. New York, NY: Oxford University Press, 2005.

Roger Hood and Carolyn Hoyle, *The Death Penalty: A Worldwide Perspective*. Oxford, London: Oxford University Press, 2015.

Ivan Šimonovic, *Moving Away from the Death Penalty Arguments, Trends and Perspectives*. United Nations, 2014.

Charles S. Lanier, William J. Bowers, and James R. Acker, *The Future of America's Death Penalty: An Agenda for the next Generation of Capital Punishment Research*. Durham, NC: Carolina Academic, 2009.

Evan J. Mandery, *Capital Punishment in America: A Balanced Examination*. Sudbury, MA: Jones and Bartlett, 2013.

Mario Marazziti, *13 Ways of Looking at the Death Penalty*. New York, NY Seven Stories, 2015.

Peggy J Parks, *Does the Death Penalty Deter Crime?* San Diego, CA: ReferencePoint, 2010.

Periodicals and Internet Sources

Frank R. Baumgartner and Betsy Neill, "Does the Death Penalty Target People Who Are Mentally Ill? We Checked." *The Washington Post*, April 3, 2017.

"The Case Against the Death Penalty." *American Civil Liberties Union*. ACLU.

Ta-Nehisi Coates, "The Inhumanity of the Death Penalty." *The Atlantic*, May 12, 2014.

Andrew Cohen, "What Americans Don't Understand About the Death Penalty." *The Atlantic*, October 30, 2013.

Joel Cohen, Richard A. Posner, and Jed S. Rakoff, "What the Travesty in Arkansas Tells Us About the Possibility for a Just Death Penalty in America." *Slate Magazine*, April 28, 2017.

Maura Dolan, "Trying to Speed up Executions Could Deal 'mortal Blow' to California Supreme Court." *Los Angeles Times*, April 2, 2017.

David Von Drehle, "Capital Punishment: The End of the Death Penalty." *Time*, June 8, 2015.

The Editorial Board, "The Death Penalty, Nearing Its End." *The New York Times*, October 24, 2016.

Philip Holloway, "Death Penalty: Why America Needs a Rethink." *CNN*, July 26, 2015.

Jeff Jacoby, "Capital Punishment Serves a Purpose." *BostonGlobe.com.*

Rebecca McCray, "The Long—but Necessary—Process to Execute Death Row Inmates Is Itself Cruel." *Slate Magazine*, March 7, 2017.

Brian Melley, "California Gives Lifeline to Death Penalty, Approves Reform." *U.S. News & World Report*, November 23, 2016.

David B. Muhlhausen, "How the Death Penalty Saves Lives." *U.S. News & World Report*, September 29, 2014.

Robert T. Muller, "Death Penalty May Not Bring Peace to Victims' Families." *Psychology Today.* Sussex Publishers, October 19, 2016.

"Part I: History of the Death Penalty." *History of the Death Penalty. Death Penalty Information Center.*

"Part II: History of the Death Penalty." *History of the Death Penalty. Death Penalty Information Center.*

Jeffrey Toobin, "Cruel And Unusual." *The New Yorker*, May 8, 2017.

Index

A

abolitionist movement, 7
Alito, Justice Samuel, 68, 70
American Medical
    Association (AMA), 61,
    63, 76, 78–79, 82
American Pharmacist
    Association (APhA), 81–87

B

Babbitt, Bill, 98
Baze v. Rees, 62
Beckett, Katherine, 33–40
Beylor, Craig, 93–94
Blecker, Robert, 69, 70, 71
Bloodsworth, Kirk, 102
Boehnlein, James K., 61–65
Breyer, Justice Stephen, 68
Burge, David, 69, 71

C

Capital Punishment in
    Context, 50–60
Chapman, Jay, 86, 87
Code of Medical Ethics, 63
Colson, Nicole, 88–95
compounding pharmacies,
    83–84, 85
Criminal Justice Legal
    Foundation, 71
Culp-Ressler, Tara, 81–87

D

Davis, Troy, 95
death penalty
    abroad, 29–32, 108–110
    administered to the
        innocent, 88–95, 104–
        106
    attempts to "fix," 104–107
    and closure, 12
    compared to life
        imprisonment, 15–16
    cost of, 26–28, 105
    cruelty of, 13–15
    as a deterrent, 11, 13, 19–20
    and gender bias, 45–49
    history of, 7–9, 37–38
    hypocrisy of, 12–13
    impact on families, 96–103
    as ineffective deterrent, 12,
        29–32
    and issues of legal
        misrepresentation, 50–60
    and medical ethics, 61–65,
        82–83, 85–86
    as only punishment for
        murder, 16
    in pop culture, 22–25
    as preventing reform of
        criminals, 10–11, 20–21
    and racial bias, 33–40
    and religion, 18, 67, 68–69

as retribution, 18–19
Death Penalty Information
    Center, 27, 47
Dieter, Richard, 27, 47
Douglas v. California, 51

E

Edloe, Leonard, 84–85
Evans, Heather, 33–40
Everett, Reverend Walter,
    101–102

F

FlameHorse, 10–16
Ford, Glenn, 72, 104–105, 106
Furman v. Georgia, 34, 36, 37,
    38, 40, 69

G

Gacy, John Wayne, 14
Gideon v. Wainwright, 51
Gilbert, Elizabeth, 92
Ginsburg, Justice Ruth Bader,
    68
Gissendaner, Kelly, 45, 46, 47,
    48
Glazer, Steven, 59, 60
Glossip v. Gross, 67, 69, 70, 72
Graham, Gary, 53–55
Grann, David, 88, 90, 91, 92,
    93, 94
Green Mile, The, 22–25
Gregory, Tim, 91
Grigson, James, 91–92
Gursel, Akim, 55, 56

H

Hippocratic Oath, 65, 82
Hood, Roger, 29–32
Howard, Jeffrey, 17–21
Hoyle, Carolyn, 29–32
Hurst, Gerald, 92–93
Hyden, Marc, 104–107

I

International Covenant on
    Civil and Political Rights,
    32

J

Jackson, John, 90, 91, 92
Jenkins, Tricia, 59
Jones, Sandra, 100, 101

K

Kauffman, Kelsey, 82, 83, 94,
    87

L

legal representation
    effectiveness of, 52
    issues of, 53–60
    right to, 50–52
    standards of, 52
lethal injection, 9, 17, 26,
    61–65, 81, 82, 99
    difficulty finding drugs for,
        83–85, 86–87, 106
    inhumanity of, 73–79
    legality of, 67–72

M

Mayyasi, Alex, 26–28
McCarthy, Matt, 85–86
McGuire, Dennis, 81–82, 83
McWee, Celia, 96–98, 99, 101
Memon, Yakub, 17
Mikulich, Alex, 68, 71
Mock, Ron, 53, 54, 94
Moussaoui, Zacarias, 16
Murder Victims' Families for
  Human Rights, 98, 99, 101
Murray v. Giarratano, 51

N

National Coalition to Abolish
  the Death Penalty, 68, 72
Newton, Frances, 94

O

Ogletree Jr., Charles, 37
Oliver, Amanda, 45–49

P

Porter, Anthony, 55–58
Powell v. Alabama, 61

R

Rappaport, Elizabeth, 48
Rompilla v. Beard, 52
Rosenberg, Alyssa, 22–25

S

Salgado, Soli, 67–72
Scheidegger, Kent, 71

Sheedy, Michael, 70
sodium thiopental, 14, 62, 74
Stoicescu, Claudia, 31
Streib, Victor, 47
Strickland v. Washington, 52,
  55, 56
Supreme Court, 26, 27, 37, 45,
  50, 51, 52, 55, 56, 58, 59,
  62, 67, 68, 71, 72, 74, 75,
  79, 87, 88, 94, 95

U

United Nations, 8, 14, 99, 109
United States Government
  Accountability Office
  (GAO), 37–38
Universal Declaration of
  Human Rights, 8, 14, 108
US v. Jackson, 8

V

Valabrega, Federica, 96–103
Viasna, 108–110

W

Warden, Rob, 103
Wiggins v. Smith, 52
Williams v. Taylor, 52
Willingham, Cameron Todd,
  88–94, 95
Witherspoon v. Illinois, 8
Wuornos, Aileen, 50, 58–60

Z

Zivot, Joel B., 73–79, 85